The Perils of Toxic Leadership

By Dr. Chris Justino

DORRANCE
PUBLISHING CO
EST. 1920
PITTSBURGH, PENNSYLVANIA 15238

Dorrance Publishing Co
585 Alpha Drive
Suite 103
Pittsburgh, PA 15238
Visit our website at *www.dorrancebookstore.com*

ISBN: 979-8-88812-125-2
eISBN: 979-8-88812-625-7

Acknowledgments

I am deeply indebted to everyone who took the time to participate in my study and provide input that helped satisfy a true knowledge gap. A special thanks to my friends who have been here every step of the way, constantly checking in on the progress and keeping me honest on my timelines. I am forever grateful for your encouragement and thoughtfulness.

I want to thank every leader I have ever worked for, under, and around. Whether the experience was positive or negative, I came out learning more than I walked in with. In the end, I believe every experience justifies our existence at a human level and could make us better if we choose to learn from it. Toxic leaders, poor workplace cultures, and employees feeling the need to quit their workplace is a momentary affliction in the grand scheme of life but provides a lifetime of lessons. Those lessons helped me complete the foundational study and dissertation that led to this book while guiding me through every leadership decision in business and in life. If we don't use these lessons to be better, then we never have the ability to provide a better existence for those that come after us. That better existence is the only thing that matters.

Lastly and most importantly I could not have undertaken this journey without my family. I want to thank Mom for showing me the power of education all those years ago and my dad, who championed me through this tedious process. I want to thank my sister and brother for their support and helping me keep up my motivation. To the mother of my children, you always supported me in my academic endeavors and continue to push me to be better. Finally, I want to thank my two little boys for being perfect, making me laugh when I need it, and for your patience and understanding throughout this time-consuming experience.

Abstract

The role of a leader is to be the conductor of an ensemble, an individual who sees the larger picture and puts the pieces of the puzzle together to obtain that picture. The positive leader finds the hidden talents of those they employ and provide the best footing for those talents to prosper and add to the overall value of the product being produced. When it comes to a negative or toxic leader, keeping employees engaged and in their roles long enough to achieve a final product becomes much of an effort and expense. In this book, toxic leadership refers to a leader who displays traits such as abusive supervision, authoritarian leadership, narcissism, unpredictability, and self-promotion.

This type of leader is associated with creating a hostile work environment that leads to employee dissatisfaction, disengagement, demotivation, and ultimately the intent to leave their role. This book, based off of my quantitative cross-sectional non-experimental study explores the relationship between the five toxic leadership traits, employee turnover intentions, and whether that relationship is affected by different cultural typologies (workplace cultures). This original study garnered a total of 613 survey respondents who were at least 18 years of age and in their role for more than one year.

The study findings show a significant relationship among all five toxic leadership traits with turnover intention and that the relationship is so significant that it negates any influence by the cultural typologies on employees' turnover intentions. This book is of great interest to anyone who considers themselves a leader. Any leader should constantly wish to better themselves for their people, and for themselves. Learning foundational knowledge is a step towards being better.

Contents

Chapter 1: Introduction

Business psychologists and social scientists are increasingly focusing on toxic leadership and its associated toxic traits and behaviors (Bakkal et al., 2019; Leet, 2011; Matos et al., 2018; Schmidt, 2008). Toxic leadership, as defined by Schmidt (2008), is a multi-faceted construct that encapsulates five distinct traits that hinder an employee's ability to be productive and perform their job while also harming their engagement and job satisfaction. This type of leadership has the potential to adversely affect not only subordinates within an organization but the entirety of an organizational culture itself (Boddy, 2013; Lipman-Blumen, 2005).

More recent and prominent examples of toxic leaders include individuals like Jeff Skilling of Enron Corporation, who advocated for free trade and opened the energy markets, completely reinventing Wall Street and Main Street, or Steve Jobs of Apple Incorporated, who helped make it possible to condense 1,000 songs onto a singular handheld device (Isaacson, 2015). These men changed history, the way people live, and how business is conducted. Despite their stature as titans who have built companies towering over many developing countries, they have also altered the means of human progress by their toxicity. Skilling built Enron Corporation, destroyed the company in less than a decade, and defrauded millions of people of their livelihoods (McLean & Elkind, 2013). Jobs created a work of art through technology, but he also ruled Apple with an iron fist and, through sheer force, alienated dozens of his one-time friends and employees (Isaacson, 2015).

Not all toxic leaders sit at the helm of flagship organizations, and not all can wreak havoc on such a grand economic scale (McClear, 2019). The aforementioned men are just a small example of a rampant issue that currently exists in all organization types, and the problem seems to be growing (Rosen et al., 2016). Although these are examples of leaders in executive positions who have far-reaching organizational influence, toxic leaders exist at all levels of management and supervision in various organizations.

According to a 2017 *Life Meets Work* study on the effects of toxic work environments in the United States, 56% of American workers have endured a toxic leader, and 73% of employee turnover results from a toxic leader (Lazarczyk, 2017). In a similar study (Singh et al., 2018), toxic leadership was responsible for a 48% decrease in work effort and a 38% decrease in work quality in the United States alone. The Conference Board estimated that employee disengagement from work due to a toxic leader costs companies between $450 billion and $500 billion U.S. annually (Jahn, 2020). Regarding workplace incivility, a common dynamic in toxic work environments, the typical loss to the average business is upwards of $14,500 per employee annually (Johnson et al., 2016). A toxic culture can lead to upwards of a 50% involuntary turnover rate and costs roughly 20% of an employee's salary to replace the worker (Bouchey & Glynn, 2012). These facts point to a seemingly obvious dynamic: Toxic leadership negatively affects the workplace and workforce.

This study measured Schmidt's (2008) five traits of toxic leadership, which include: (a) abusive supervision, (b) authoritarian leadership, (c) narcissism, (d) self-promotion, and (e) unpredictability. These traits were tested with Cameron's and Quinn's (1999) four organizational cultural typologies, which include: (a) clan cultures, (b) hierarchical cultures, (c) market cultures, and (d) adhocracy cultures. In this study, I identified relationships between toxic traits and turnover intention, and toxic traits and turnover intention within individual cultural typologies. Specific Human Resources Management (HRM) functions, such as hiring, promoting, employee development, changes in management, and succession planning, are considered part of HRM efforts toward continuous organizational development and improvement. This chapter presents background information on this topic and outlines my exploration of the aforementioned typologies to further the research on toxic work cultures.

Background

Social science research (Resick et al., 2013; Schlaegel et al., 2020) on leadership appears to focus on topics that provide insight into what makes a successful leader. The current scientific literature (Haslam et al., 2011;

Savage-Austin & Honeycutt, 2011) on leadership seems to focus mainly on the positive aspects of leadership and how best to achieve goals by championing and developing people. In some cases, a charismatic leader may have the ability to lead an organization from the front and have followers support their every move. In other cases, a leader needs to have courage and commitment to the cause yet allow their employees to take charge of their destiny in a transformational way. Perhaps great leaders are born with the right combination of ability and genetics and lead by some sort of divine inspiration.

Subordinates prefer leaders to have emotional intelligence while providing an open and safe environment for all employees to work and be authentic to who they are (Schlaegel et al., 2020). The science of the nature-versus-nurture debate is ongoing and evolving but has led to numerous studies (Borgatta et al., 1954; Hoppe, 2007; Schlaegel et al., 2020) that seek to decipher what specific traits HRM professionals should look for in a strong and capable leader. The science of understanding the negative aspects of leadership is fragmented at best when compared to the science of the positive effects of leadership on organizational development.

On the largest scale, the world witnessed firsthand how toxic leadership can endanger the wellbeing of many workers during the 2008 financial crisis (Heppell, 2011). However, the topic of toxic leadership is typically not present in the public consciousness without the help of a major external event, such as the last financial collapse, although it continues to exist and cause harm. Unfortunately, toxic leadership is most often discussed during times of calamity (Heppell, 2011; Hoppe, 2007).

Toxic Leadership

Schmidt (2008) defined toxic leadership as a multi-faceted construct that encapsulates five distinct traits, which both hinder an employee's ability to work productively and harm their engagement and job satisfaction and which have been exemplified by leaders who are regarded as toxic. Schmidt's scale of measurement measures five distinct traits: (a) abusive supervision, (b) authoritarian leadership, (c) narcissism, (d) self-promotion, and (e) unpredictability.

According to Schmidt (2014):

Abusive supervision appears in a conniving, manipulative, and/or humiliating leader who draws a negative response.

Authoritarian leadership derives from the micromanaging of employees or subordinates and the lack of empowerment that stems from this type of environment.

Narcissism in a leader often takes away from the employee by minimizing their ability or work while inflating the ability and work of the leader.

Self-promotion in a leader diminishes employees' value while inflating the leader's value.

Unpredictability is defined as an extremely varied personality that can sometimes be described as caring and nurturing in one instance and volatile and potentially violent in other instances.

These traits signify toxic tendencies that, individually or in combination, create a toxic work or organizational environment. This typically leads employees not to care for their roles and work due to a lack of emotional or structural support and employee disengagement. Finally, this type of culture can lead to high employee turnover intention that can prove costly to an organization (Bakkal et al., 2019).

Cultural Typologies

Social scientists have defined cultural typologies based on how a business organization is designed to operate as influenced by internal and external forces (Cameron & Quinn, 1999; Denison, 2019). Cameron and Quinn (1999) worked on cultural typologies and utilized four common workplace cultures. In their model (see Figure 1), they suggested that modern-day organizational cultures stem from four foundational typologies: (a) clan culture, (b) hierarchical culture, (c) market culture, and (d) adhocracy culture. These cultures are situated within a two- dimension framework, known as either the Competing Values Culture Model or Competing Values Framework, which considers control versus flexibility and internal versus external dynamics.

For the vertical axis, control insinuates the amount of control an employee endures within a culture. The flexibility derives from the amount the employee can operate with minimal oversight. For the horizontal axis, internal dynamics regard the organization's intent and culture as built from within the organization. External dynamics suggest the organizational culture is built from the outside (e.g., clients, customers, and external stakeholders). Clan cultures adhere to flexibility while focusing on the internal team. Hierarchical cultures also focus on the internal team or organization but emphasize control and structure. Market cultures look to the external environment and use those parameters for their sense of control and structure. Finally, adhocracies give control to the individual and emphasize creativity (Cameron & Quinn, 1999).

The Competing Values Framework

Cultural typologies exist based on different dynamics. They can be restrictive and regimented or open and promote employee decision-making to provide greater opportunities for creativity. While each typology may influence employees' intentions to leave the working environment (e.g., the organization), no literature discusses the relationship between toxic leadership traits and organizational cultural typologies on turnover intentions. Despite the two- dimensional values associated with these typologies, I did not measure these dimensions in my study. Instead, I focused entirely on typology as a moderator for the relationship between toxic leadership traits and employee turnover intentions.

Turnover Intentions

Turnover intentions, whether they result from a perceived toxic environment or not, result from an extremely problematic corporate culture and environment (Roodt, 2013). Employee turnover is common in organizations, but it can be a troublesome phenomenon when it occurs at a high percentage of the total employee population. When an employee endures an emotionally or physically unsafe workplace environment, the only potential change the employee can make to their situation is to escape it. As time passes and the employee is unable to find a suitable alternative to help them cope, resentment sets in and reinforces their negative mindset, thereby providing a foundation for employee disengagement, disenfranchisement, and disloyalty (Roodt, 2013; Seppalaa & Cameron, 2015). During their research on turnover intentions, Roodt (2013) found that the intent of an employee to leave their current job can be just as detrimental as an employee who leaves their role or organization; the costs associated with employee disengagement and diminished performance had damaging consequences for organizations, especially if turnover intentions fester over time.

Problem Statement

The problem is that toxic leadership traits and cultural typologies may each hurt employee attitudes and performance; however, no evidence measured the correlation between individual toxic leadership traits and employee turnover intentions or suggested how cultural typologies may mediate the effects of toxic leadership on employee turnover intentions. The literature (Bakkal et al., 2019; Boddy, 2013; Chen et al., 2020; Heppell, 2011; Reed, 2004) suggested toxic leadership is a problem but did not identify specific traits or state which toxic leadership traits have a stronger relationship with employee turnover intentions, especially within each cultural typology. Another problem is that there was little evidence of how others in an organization can identify toxic leaders before they enter senior-level positions, where they have the power to revamp an entire organizational culture and replace it with one filled with fear, deceit, anxiety and, ultimately, demotivated employees who show diminished productivity (Seppalaa & Cameron, 2015).

Significance of the Study/Research Contribution

Earlier studies (Bakkal et al., 2019; Boddy, 2013; Matos et al., 2018) looked at leadership's negative or dark sides, and their findings offered insight into leadership toxicity and its potential effects on the workplace. There is readily available research (Bakkal et al., 2019; Matos et al., 2018; Schmidt, 2008) on toxic leadership that provides strong foundational knowledge for this study. Many researchers (Audi & Murphy, 2006; Haslam et al., 2011; Hoppe, 2007; Lindebaum & Cartwright, 2010) focused on what "right leadership" looks like, but in my purview, the traits defined by this approach are purely relative and can be interchangeable. If the focus is on the traits that define toxic leadership, HRM should be given the tools to identify these traits when they conduct their day-to-day operations. In this study, a leader was considered any individual with authority over subordinates in an organization. Leaders can hold positions from those just below the C-suite (e.g., executive-level) or include the lowest level, supervisors.

Understanding the effects of toxic leadership traits concerning the organizational cultural typology in which toxic leaders' function can be valuable tools for HRM professionals to perform their jobs. Exploring the effects and specific traits of toxic leadership can profoundly affect HRM and corporate culture as a whole. By viewing the phenomenon through a scientific lens, I initially hoped to identify the toxic leadership traits most strongly related to employee turnover intentions and influenced by the prevailing cultural typology within a workplace. In the study, I explored the correlation between toxic leadership traits and employee turnover intentions and whether there was a further correlation with specific cultural typologies. With the results, I was able to add to the current literature and help fill gaps related to toxic leadership in different cultural typologies.

Definition of Terms

Abusive supervision in this study entails the emotional distress of an employee that stems from a leader that can be portrayed as conniving, manipulative, and/or humiliating (Schmidt, 2014). The abuse is intended by the abuser to draw a negative response from the abused.

Adhocracy culture alludes to a culture based on energy and creativity that allows employees to take risks and enjoy latitude and freedom of movement (Cameron & Quinn, 1999).

Authoritarian leadership derives from the micromanaging of employees or subordinates and the lack of empowerment that stems from this type of environment (Schmidt, 2008).

Clan culture is defined as a culture that is more similar to a family. Leaders are mentors, communication and teamwork are paramount, and relationships between employees and customers are quite valuable (Cameron & Quinn, 1999).

Cultural typology, as defined by Cameron and Quinn (1999), describes a typical workplace environment or culture. The four cultural typologies used within this study are adhocracy, clan culture, market culture, and hierarchical culture.

Hierarchical culture is defined as an organizational culture that is built on control and structure. The environment is formal, efficient, predictable, and consistent. There is not much ability for freedom and expression (Cameron & Quinn, 1999).

Job satisfaction relates to feelings of enjoyment, motivation, and contentment in an employee's work or role. Job satisfaction is accompanied by a sense of stability, the possibility to progress in one's career, and comfort in one's work and personal life (Roodt, 2013).

Market culture is built upon the dynamics of achievement and competition. The leaders are tough and demanding, and success is the only option (Cameron & Quinn, 1999).

Narcissism stems from the perceived greatness the toxic leader believes they portray. This trait often reduces the employee by minimizing their abilities or work while inflating the abilities and work of the leader (Schmidt, 2008).

Self-promotion alludes to the leader's inability to take the blame for negative dynamics or outcomes, but their ability to take praise for the positive dynamics and outcomes (Schmidt, 2008). This trait diminishes the value of employees while inflating that of the leader.

Toxic leadership is a leadership behavior that portrays poor decision-making skills that best suit the leader's ego and ambition to progress either economically or positionally while spreading a culture of distrust, disenfranchisement, and disengagement, leading to high turnover among the employees and subordinates. This definition aligns with that of Schmidt (2008) and includes the toxic leadership traits of: (a) abusive supervision, (b) authoritarian leadership, (c) narcissism, (d) self-promotion, and (e) unpredictability.

Turnover intention is an employee's intent to leave their current role or position by beginning the search for a new role while still actively employed (Roodt, 2013).

Unpredictability is defined as an extremely varied personality that can be described as caring and nurturing in one instance and volatile and potentially violent in other instances. The employee never truly knows what to expect on a minute-by-minute basis (Schmidt, 2008).

Conceptual Model

The five key traits, as described by Schmidt (2008), were the baseline independent variables that I focused on and were used to predict the overall outcome of the dependent variable: employee turnover intention. In the study, I endeavored to find the correlation between Schmidt's toxic leadership traits and employee turnover intentions as moderated by cultural typologies defined by the Cultural Typology Model outlined by Cameron and Quinn (1999).

Research Questions

I answered two main questions regarding toxic leadership traits, the four cultural typologies, and employee turnover intentions:

• Do each of the five toxic leadership traits significantly affect turnover intention?

• If so, are those effects moderated by cultural typologies?

Hypotheses

H1a. Abusive supervision adversely affects the turnover intentions of employees working in each of the four cultural typologies to varying degrees.

N1a. Abusive supervision does not affect the turnover intentions of employees working in each of the four cultural typologies to varying degrees.

H1b. Authoritarian leadership adversely affects the turnover intentions of employees working in each of the four cultural typologies to varying degrees.

N1b. Authoritarian leadership does not affect the turnover intentions of employees working in each of the four cultural typologies to varying degrees.

H1c. Narcissism adversely affects the turnover intentions of employees working in each of the four cultural typologies to varying degrees.

N1c. Narcissism does not affect the turnover intentions of employees working in each of the four cultural typologies to varying degrees.

H1d. Self-promotion adversely affects the turnover intentions of employees working in each of the four cultural typologies to varying degrees.

N1d. Self-promotion does not affect the turnover intentions of employees working in each of the four cultural typologies to varying degrees.

H1e. Unpredictability adversely affects the turnover intentions of employees working in each of the four cultural typologies to varying degrees.

N1e. Unpredictability does not affect the turnover intentions of employees working in each of the four cultural typologies to varying degrees.

Testing the toxic leadership traits Schmidt (2008) identified in his Toxic Leadership Scale against the Turnover Intention Scale by Roodt (2013) sought to identify toxic leadership traits that most frequently result in extreme employee dissatisfaction in each cultural typology.

Methodology

Using the shortened version of the Schmidt (2008) Toxic Leadership Scale, the study tested employee perception of five common toxic leadership traits about the employees' intent to leave their current roles, which I measured with the shortened Turnover Intention Scale (TIS-6) from Roodt (2013). The ideal categorical sample was a minimum sample size of 148 participants. A medium effect size of 0.50 ensured the strength of the relationships between variables was not overly strict or lenient (Faul et al., 2007). The intent was to analyze whether or not there was a relationship between the individual toxic leadership traits outlined by Schmidt (2008)—(a) abusive supervision, (b) narcissism, (c) authoritative leadership, (d) self-promotion, and (e) unpredictability—and employee turnover intentions Roodt (2013) noted in the TIS-6.

Using linear regression analysis, I was able to examine whether or not the predictors (toxic leadership traits) had an effect on the outcome (i.e., turnover intentions) and used the coefficient to test the strength of that initial correlation. To test the outcome against the Moderating Variable (MV) (i.e., culture typology), I dummy-coded the four cultural typologies by creating an interaction term within the SPSS ® Software (IBM, 2022). Using a 2-way Univariate Model, I analyzed how the specific toxic leadership traits and their relationships with turnover intention were affected by a moderating variable of culture typology.

Assumptions

There are aspects of the study that I simply could not know but that I assumed to be accurate. The initial assumption was that the participants were open, honest, and willing to share their thoughts truthfully on the surveys. Another assumption was that they were able to answer the survey in a self-provided safe space to secure trust and honest answers from the participants. It was also safe to assume that the data provided feedback on underlying psychological connections and that the quantitative survey was vast enough to provide such feedback. I also assumed that each participant understood the questions as designed and answered with that understanding.

The assumption about the individuals who worked in toxic environments and their participation was that employee turnover intention is the final stage of an employee's ability to maintain their role due to the stresses of toxic leadership or a toxic culture. In this study, I also assumed that lower-level workers were affected by senior-to-executive-level toxic leaders who may not be their direct supervisors. All leaders below a C-suite position were assumed to be affected by toxic leadership. Also, I assumed toxicity existed in all types of organizations and cultures. Finally, I assumed that a connection with toxic leadership affects turnover intentions.

Limitations

The study was not all-encompassing and had weaknesses that may have impacted and influenced the data collected or its interpretation and analysis. Of course, assuming the truth in a participant's answer was also a limitation. The data relied on the truthfulness of a participant's response, and the limitation was simply that I would never truly know if the participants portrayed the truth. It is also worth noting that an individual's personality may have affected their surroundings, perceptions, and interactions between the leader and subordinate. Regarding personality-driven conflict, I assumed that today's culture and cultural affiliations may have skewed perceptions and could negatively affect the data. Furthermore, the data may have been skewed through the social acceptability of the participants' responses in an attempt to conform to groupthink.

This study did not pinpoint responses from specific-level managers (e.g., low-level, mid- level, or senior-level leaders), but it excluded executive-level leaders. The study collected data on various workplaces, such as the corporate or private sector, government or public sector, or military environment. However, it did not differentiate toxic leadership types within those workplaces, and I did not use the data in the final analysis. There was a collection of demographical information but no data analyses of the responses. Responses to demographic questions identified age, gender, level of education, time in the current role, ethnicity, and type of work (e.g., government, non-profit, for-profit, and military). This information was useful to determine if participants represented the general population after the data collection.

The decision not to differentiate between or analyze specific characteristics prevented me from distinguishing the differences and nuances between these factors. Finally, due to the COVID-19 pandemic, changes in work rules and dynamics may have affected participants' responses and the study outcome. By accepting participants who work from remote locations, the distance between the toxic leaders and the participants may have affected the impact of the participants' responses.

I was only concerned with perceived toxicity that stems from any leader or manager in the participants' workplace and the overall effects those toxic traits have on the participants regarding turnover intention. In this study, I was not concerned with any participant who operated in an executive role or had not worked for at least one year in their current workplace where their perceived toxic environment was reported to persist.

Due to the nature of quantitative methodology, participants' answers were replaced with numerals, which tends to obscure the "why" of an answer. Although I did not conduct interviews after the survey was completed due to time constraints and the nature of the study design, there is a concern that with a purely quantitative methodology the research may have led to actual or perceived confirmation bias (McLeod, 2019). Finally, social desirability and conformity bias may have skewed the results, as participants may have answered questions in a manner that others would view favorably.

Delimitations

Due to the scope of the study, there were external factors that I have not included. This research attempted to define and test the strength of the relationship between the five toxic traits against the turnover intention and to see if culture typologies affected those relationships. By doing so, I gained an understanding of those relationships and saw whether certain traits were more harmful when testing against culture typologies. In this study, I only considered the four typologies Cameron and Quinn (1999) presented and did not consider other typology models published by other researchers. I also did not consider other possibly toxic traits that can harm an employee or a subordinate in a perceived toxic environment and only utilized the traits identified in the Schmidt (2008) validated scale of measurement. This study used a Likert scale for the quantitative approach; each validated scale was used to collect data and did not expand on the reasoning for the participants' answers via a mixed-method or qualitative approach.

Summary

Toxic leadership is a systemic issue that has not been alleviated through past studies or other forms of leadership. I believe there are significant information gaps in the study of toxic leadership and its overall effects on organizational culture. There was plenty of written history and examples of extreme toxic cultures shaped by the leadership, as seen in the Enron Corporation, Apple Incorporated, and Wells Fargo & Co., but there were far less scientific literature by academics and practitioners to combat the problem.

Cultures led by toxic leaders still exist and flourish despite the seemingly endless amount of data on positive leadership. I, therefore, sought to understand the effects of overall organizational toxicity stemming from senior-level leaders. The study was backed by the latest scientific research and used currently validated scales of measurement. It tested the five toxic leadership traits in the four cultural typologies. I intended to produce quantitatively driven data to test the strength of the relationship between the five toxic traits against the turnover intention and to see if culture typologies affected those relationships.

This chapter has offered background information to build a foundation for the problem. It introduced the notions of toxic leadership, cultural typologies, and turnover intentions, discussed the study's significance, defined the terms, and outlined its potential contribution to existing research and the literature. Finally, it identified the study's assumptions, limitations, and delimitations. In the next chapter, I discuss existing literature on toxic leadership and expand on the ideas presented in Chapter 1.

Chapter 2: Literature Review

The purpose of this quantitative study was to thoroughly analyze the five major traits of a toxic leader against the four defined cultural typologies using employee turnover intention as the result of a leader's toxicity. The intent was to identify and rank the traits in the cultural typologies from most to least detrimental, as the employees perceive them, test the strength of the relationship between the five toxic traits against the turnover intention, and see if culture typologies affected those relationships. The research suggested a strong correlation between toxic leaders, the culture they perpetuate, and employee dissatisfaction. However, there are glaring gaps in the literature that fail to give HRM specific guidance as to which traits were deemed worse or more offensive to employees who work in the different cultural typologies.

The Research

During the research process, I used various sources to compile a master list of documents and support for this dissertation. These included the Touro Library, Google Scholar, *Academia.edu,* and Microsoft Academic. I focused specifically on academic writing and research conducted in the last ten years, although several referenced materials were substantially older and have maintained their original findings throughout the years. The references cited include 26 scientific studies, 19 research articles from professional journals, and 5 monographs that provide the foundational support for this work on toxic leadership. The Boolean search compiled works on both negative and positive leadership traits and their effects on organizational culture, the specific scales of measurements used to identify leadership qualities and their effects, and historical portrayals of failed or negative leadership.

Specific key phrases I used in the Boolean search included "toxic leadership," "negative leadership," and "traits associated with leaders." For the positive side of leadership, I used

phrases like "positive leadership," "great leadership," and "successful leadership." I also used key phrases that touched upon organizational cultures, such as "organizational typologies" and "organizational culture," along with key phrases that discussed various behaviors and workplace systems. Finally, I used phrases like "employee behavior," "employee satisfaction," "employee engagement," and "employee morale" to review the scientific literature on how employees react to the aforementioned types of leaders. Combining these phrases in a Boolean search allowed me to perform a simplified yet targeted review of the latest information on the topic.

The literature for this study focused on the factual effects of toxic leadership, negative leadership, and positive leadership to compare past academic work and build a foundation for this study and future studies. The major professional journals I used included the *Leadership & Organization Development Journal*, the *Journal of Business Ethics*, the *Journal of Human Resource Management*, *Social Behavior and Personality: An International Journal*, the *Journal of Applied Psychology*, the *Journal of Management Studies*, *Personnel Psychology*, the *Journal of Business & Economics Research*, and *Harvard Business Review*. The major themes I identified include the effects of toxic leadership, the effects of healthy leadership, cultural typologies, turnover intentions, job satisfaction, perceptions of organizational justice, and the costs of toxic leadership.

Toxic Leadership

Toxic leadership is one of the most intricate and cumbersome problems affecting Americans' everyday lives today. Whether the issue stems from an unpredictable and narcissistic leader who occupies the office of the President, or an abusive supervisor at the local ice cream shop, the effects can have damning consequences on the subordinates (Heppell, 2011; Schmidt, 2008). Toxic leaders have been known to crush individuals' spirits, break up unit-level teams,

dismantle entire businesses and organizations, and singlehandedly dismantle decades' worth of international relations (Chen et al., 2020; Comey, 2018; Farrell, 2011). The costs associated with toxic leadership can be vast.

Toxic workplace cultures have cost U.S. companies over $223 billion from 2014 to 2019, have caused 1 in 5 American workers to leave their roles, and 49% of employees have considered leaving their organizations due to toxic cultures (McClear, 2019).

Toxic leadership is a leadership behavior in which a leader's decision-making process is based solely on their ambition and ego as they seek to progress either economically or positionally (the ambitious upward movement through the organization to gain seniority and/or power) as they spread a culture of distrust, disenfranchisement, and disengagement among the subordinates (Schmidt, 2008). In addition to Schmidt's extensive work, which introduced a valid scale by which to measure toxic leadership, other researchers have also studied the topic, including Lipman-Blumen (2005), who focused on political leaders, Reed (2004, 2015), who focused on leaders in the military, and Bakkal et al. (2019), who focused on healthcare leadership. Although this study focused on Schmidt's toxic leadership traits and his Toxic Leadership Scale, exploring other work on the subject is also important.

Schmidt's Validated Scale on Toxic Leadership

Schmidt (2008) recognized the media's emphasis on toxic leadership but realized there was little scientific study on the subject. When he began his research, the traits other researchers used to describe toxic or dysfunctional leadership were not uniform, and there was no formal measurement scale. Schmidt used the most cited articles of the time, compiled a list of traits to describe toxic leadership, and tested them in a multidimensional study. The first part of the study defined and codified themes around the traits through focus groups and interviews with 23

U.S. military personnel. The second part of the study took the traits he derived from the qualitative themes and tested them in a questionnaire format on 218 undergraduate students from a large mid-Atlantic university (Schmidt, 2008). From this, Schmidt created a validated scale of measurement by identifying and ranking the themes and producing the top five traits associated with toxic leadership.

Schmidt (2008) identified five key traits of a toxic leader in his validated Toxic Leadership Scale, including: (a) abusive supervision, (b) authoritarian leadership, (c) narcissism,

(d) self-promotion, and (e) unpredictability. Schmidt (2008) focused on locating and defining the traits that employees deemed the most aligned with their perceptions of a toxic leader. The multidimensional study used individuals in both military and civilian capacities to refine the study on toxic leadership traits and helped develop the scale to help predict employee dissatisfaction.

Abusive Supervision

Abusive supervision is the emotional distress of an employee that stems from a leader who is conniving, manipulative, and/or humiliating (Schmidt, 2014). An abusive supervisor typically reverts to public humiliation, extreme aggression or passive-aggressiveness, and emotional swings (i.e., daily unpredictability). The emotion that stems from this trait is usually fear, which leaves an employee unmotivated, dissatisfied, and untrusting of not only the leader but also of fellow employees (Schmidt, 2008).

Authoritarian Leadership

Authoritarian leadership derives from the micromanaging of employees or subordinates and the lack of empowerment that stems from this type of environment (Schmidt, 2008). This type of leader must always have control, both when supervising the work of others and their work. Relinquishing control, no matter the subordinate's abilities, is never an option for this type of leader. If they assign tasks to the subordinates, they are typically mundane and routine items.

The authoritarian leader is the extreme version of a micromanager and typically takes praise from higher authorities but rarely relays that praise to subordinates. The emotion employees feel from this trait is usually exhaustion or fatigue, which destroys their morale and diminishes their incentive or desire to progress (Schmidt, 2008).

Narcissism

Narcissism stems from the perceived greatness the toxic leader believes they portray. This trait often detracts from employees by minimizing their abilities or work while inflating the leader's abilities and work (Schmidt, 2008). The leader takes praise from the positive feedback dictated by their leadership and, much like the authoritarian leader, never relays that positivity to the subordinates. These leaders also refuse to accept blame for negative feedback and point to a subordinate to avoid looking weak, inadequate, or wrong. A narcissistic leader also minimizes or outright denies their subordinates' suggestions, believing their ideas to be far superior (Schmidt, 2008). According to Simmons (2020), a narcissistic leader's arrogance and self-promotion would sometimes help them climb the corporate ladder and advance in the organization. However, it could also drive down organizational morale and wellbeing, eventually leading to an organizational culture permeated by arrogance, which diminishes or silences divergent voices, and is characterized by selfishness.

Self-Promotion

The self-promotion trait alludes to a leader's inability to take the blame for negative dynamics or outcomes, but their ability to take praise for all positive dynamics and outcomes (Schmidt, 2008). Like narcissistic leaders, self-promoting leaders take the credit for their teams' successes while taking none of the blame for their failures. Where the two traits diverge is in the "managing-up" facade. Self-promoting leaders provide their higher managers with a semblance of team cohesion, progress, and ability. They take the credit for the team's work and progress and portray themselves as the reason for the success. In times of hardship or failure, this leader would deflect the blame to their team or subordinates and never accept any of it for themselves. The aftereffect of such a leader may look good to their superiors but demotivates and demoralizes their subordinates (Schmidt, 2008).

Unpredictability

Schmidt (2014) found the trait of unpredictability to be present in the majority of perceived toxic leaders. These leaders act in a "hot and cold" manner, meaning that they would be nice and welcoming in one moment and angry, vicious, and standoffish in the next. This trait makes it impossible for subordinates to mitigate or manage their supervisor's expectations because of the lack of a pattern in their daily interactions. The trait leaves the employee feeling helpless, insecure, and unsafe in the workplace (Schmidt, 2008).

Lipman-Blumen's Toxic Leadership Construct

Lipman-Blumen (2005) recognized that a specific definition of a toxic leader could leave room for bias, as the idea of toxicity and the traits associated with toxicity are relative to the individual. The concern lies in the relative outlook of a toxic leader's various traits, though they may not necessarily portray all of them. Lipman-Blumen found nine traits that are common among toxic leaders: (a) a lack of integrity, (b) insatiable ambition, (c) an enormous ego, (d) arrogance, (e) amorality, (f) avarice, (g) recklessness, (h) cowardice, and (i) a failure to understand the nature of relevant problems and the ability to act competently and effectively as a leader. In Lipman-Blumen's view, a toxic leader can knowingly or unknowingly be toxic, and the consequences within a workplace culture may also differ from situation to situation. However, this type of leader always causes negative effects both during their time in power and well after it ends (Heppell, 2011).

The Lack of Integrity and Insatiable Ambition

The lack of integrity, or the inability to take responsibility for one's actions or those of the team, also extends to their inability or refusal to adhere to moral, ethical, and legal standards expected from a leader (Audi & Murphy, 2006; Lipman-Blumen, 2005). Insatiable ambition, or the constant striving for power and authority, characterizes the leader who stops at nothing to gain that power (Lipman-Blumen, 2005).

Enormous Ego and Arrogance

A leader's enormous ego and arrogance can both be subsets of the narcissism Schmidt (2008) identified, where the leader has a self-inflated view of themselves and an exaggerated deflated view of others. Additionally, the leader with an enormous ego needs an endless supply of flattery to thrive, can become unstable if the flattery ceases, and dangerous if the flattery turns negative (Lipman-Blumen, 2005). Arrogance thrives off of enormous ego and codifies the self-image of greatness while minimizing the abilities and greatness of others. The arrogant leader believes they are the smartest in the room, and only their insight is useful among their subordinates, peers, and supervisors (Lipman-Blumen, 2005).

Amorality and Avarice

Amorality touches upon the lack of integrity of a toxic leader. Along with a lack of integrity, an amoral leader ignores potential moral or ethical situations when trying to realize success or gain (Audi & Murphy, 2006; Lipman-Blumen, 2005). Avarice is an extreme version of greed, where the constant need for wealth and abundance overrides other needs and can never truly be enough for this type of leader (Lipman-Blumen, 2005).

Recklessness and Cowardice

Recklessness is a trait found in other pieces of scientific literature. Recklessness can mean a complete disregard of subordinates and their wellbeing, ethical and legal standards, precedence, and trust and dignity within an organization as a whole (Lipman-Blumen, 2005; Reed, 2004). According to Lipman-Blumen (2005), cowardice in a leader relates directly to the inability to make a decision and to paralysis when it comes to choosing what is right over what is easy or what may lead to an immediate win.

Failure to Lead

Failure to lead is the failure to understand the nature of relevant problems and the ability to act competently and effectively in all situations. This type of leader is simply not ready or unable to lead, may not have the experience or knowledge to handle issues or mitigate problems, and certainly cannot make decisions to move an entity forward (Lipman-Blumen, 2005).

Effects

The effects of these leaders pose a threat not only to the employees or subordinates who operate in a workplace but extend to the entirety of the organization, as well as the families, loved ones, and people these leaders serve (Heppell, 2011; Lipman-Blumen, 2005). Lipman-Blumen's portrayal of President George W. Bush received media attention because of the reporting on the former president's leadership, but it also provided evidence that there were various levels of toxicity among leaders. Lipman-Blumen argued that in the case of President Bush, who showcased the traits of cowardice, lack of integrity, and recklessness, the toxicity was not evil or deliberate but still had greater effects that last generations. Lipman-Blumen (2005) argued that leaders who exhibit destructive behaviors and leave a trail of harm should be considered toxic, no matter their intent (Heppell, 2011).

Lipman-Blumen's (2005) conceptual framework on toxic leadership focused on various themes or behaviors that could potentially harm a workplace. Although each of the behaviors or traits in this framework vary in their greater moral and ethical dilemmas, for the leader to be considered toxic they must always participate in destructive behaviors that leave a workplace or an organization in worse shape than before the leader assumed power. Regardless of whether the leader stifles constructive criticism, ignores incompetence, or actively engages in illicit and illegal acts, they are toxic (Lipman-Blumen, 2005). This type of definition is a useful starting point to begin a conversation about destructive leaders and the cultures they inhabit but leaves the discussion far too open to interpretation in corporate settings.

Reed's Toxic Leadership in the Military

Reed (2004) offered a far more succinct take on the traits of a toxic leader. The former U.S. Army colonel used three key traits or elements to characterize the toxic leader: (a) an apparent lack of concern for subordinates, (b) a personality that negatively affects an organization, and (c) one who is motivated by self-interest. Reed focused on military leaders and surmised that the toxic leader rose through the sheer force they imposed through their command, the fear that resonated from that force, and the ambition to succeed that not only harmed people but that blinded leaders to such harm. This type of leader greatly damages the individual, team, and entire unit while also harming their families, the mission, and the reputation of the U.S. Military (Reed, 2004).

The military case is different from that of the government and corporate leaders. The difference is in the quiet suffering of the junior leaders and subordinates who endure the climate and are unable to leave of their own will (Reed, 2015). Reed (2004) argued that the military culture, which rests on loyalty, duty, selfless service, and respect, has helped maintain toxic leaders. Other aspects that conceal this type of toxic culture come from the leaders, who depicted their command style as one that leads to success, endurance, and progress. Reed argued that the entire military culture not only allowed toxic leaders to thrive, but it might even help these leaders continuously succeed.

The three traits Reed (2004) identified offer a succinct snapshot of what one may find in a toxic leader in the military, but they also left room for interpretation. What constitutes a toxic leader in the military may not necessarily relate to a toxic leader in a corporate setting. Toxic military leadership can fester and operate nearly undetected due to the nature of military culture and the engrained indoctrination in that setting (Reed, 2015). Reed's work is expansive, scientific, and involves decades of experience.

Bakkal's Take on Toxic Leadership in Healthcare

The science of leadership has become increasingly aware of the problem of toxic leadership, especially in healthcare, where hospital employees are overworked, underpaid, and typically understaffed. The stressful environment was a breeding ground for toxicity to persist and flourish. Bakkal et al. (2019) tested the perception of toxic leadership on healthcare employees in Turkey and the effects of such leadership on turnover intentions and job satisfaction. The researchers tested four toxic traits: (a) self-seeking behaviors, (b) a negative state of mind, (c) selfishness, and (d) a lack of appreciation.

Celebi et al. (2015) used a portion of Schmidt's (2008) Toxic Leadership Scale but adapted it to create their validated scale of measurement for use in Turkey with a focus on medical institutions (Bakkal et al., 2019). The study aimed to provide a unique foundation to support future studies on the generational issues of overworked and underappreciated staff in hospitals in Turkey. Bakkal et al. found that the self-seeking trait, the negative state of mind, and the lack of appreciation played a direct role in job satisfaction and eventual turnover intentions.

Bakkal et al. (2019) initially tried to connect four separate traits of toxic leadership to employee satisfaction and turnover intentions. Their study found that only three traits had a statistically significant link to employee dissatisfaction that would lead to eventual turnover intentions. Their measurement scale was adapted from Schmidt (2008) and his Toxic Leadership Scale, which they modified to adapt to the local culture in Turkey and to work with the nuances of the Turkish healthcare environment.

Schmidt's Validated Scale

Schmidt (2008) created a validated scale of measurement for toxic leadership and identified five distinct traits that are encompassing yet descriptive. They leave no room for individual interpretation and give the community of interest a starting point for further research, as seen in the work by Bakkal et al.

(2019) on healthcare leadership in Turkey. In my study, using Schmidt's scale allowed to base my research on previously validated science tested within and outside the military for its accuracy and validity. Schmidt's scale, and the resulting traits for testing, also encapsulated the work of both Lipman-Blumen (2005) and Reed (2004).

This study adopted the Toxic Leadership Scale introduced by Schmidt (2008) due to its validity and depth. The traits utilized encompass an extensive range of toxic and destructive leadership behaviors that have been studied independently (Bakkal et al., 2019; Lipman-Blumen, 2005; Reed, 2004; Schmidt, 2008) but rarely as a collective and compiled validated scale of measurement. I believe Schmidt's Toxic Leadership Scale offered a path to the most robust results that filled the gaps in the literature.

The Gaps in Knowledge Surrounding Toxic Leadership

Lipman-Blumen (2005) argued that the definition of a toxic leader is vast but that most toxic leaders tend to portray similar traits and behaviors. Lipman-Blumen went on to define the traits and behaviors of most toxic leaders and the effects those traits have on their team, organization, and loved ones. Reed (2004) worked on toxic leaders and focused on the military, defining what toxic leaders look like and how they thrive. According to Reed, these leaders look to subordinate those around them via abusive supervision. They stop at nothing to obtain the next rank and post and to provide a positive view of their leadership to their superiors while their subordinates suffer. Finally, Schmidt (2008) provided an accurate, validated scale of measurement comprising five distinct traits of toxic leadership and how toxic leaders affect organizational culture.

All this research informs the HRM community what to look for in the leaders they choose, hire, and promote. The works of Lipman-Blumen (2005), Reed (2004), Bakkal et al. (2019), and Schmidt (2008) offered a strong foundational knowledge to codify what "wrong" looks like. However, there were gaps in the literature that impeded HRM in making those choices. For example, there were gaps in knowledge about how specific work cultures/typologies interact with toxic leadership traits and whether different workplace cultures or typologies affect specific toxic leadership traits

Cultural Typologies

One must understand the organizational culture or typology to best understand an organization and its people. The Society for Human Resource Management (SHRM, 2021) defines organizational culture as a collective ideology with a core set of values in an organization or business unit. In this definition, a strong organizational typology outlines the expectations for leadership, the right responses to changing situations, and a reward system that values employees equitably (SHRM, 2021). Cultural typologies exist based on different dynamics the leadership establishes and the organization's needs. In a typical cultural typology, organizations can be restrictive, regimented, open, and creative (Cameron & Quinn, 1999).

Cameron and Quinn's Competing Values Framework

Testing of the five traits of toxicity (Schmidt, 2008) is limited because of various workplace cultures or cultural typologies that also influence employee turnover intentions. In some typologies, abusive leadership may have proven more detrimental than the four other toxic leadership traits, but this may not have been the case in other typologies. Therefore, this research treated the various cultural typologies as a moderating variable. I used the study by Cameron and Quinn (1999) and their Organizational Cultural Typology model as the basis to study organizational culture typologies.

In their Competing Values Framework, Cameron and Quinn (1999) set out to define typologies of corporate culture to adequately research the expectations within those cultures and how to address the problems that stemmed from them. To define the four cultural typologies, they tested six characteristics of an organization: dominant characteristics, organizational glue, organizational leadership, the management of employees, strategic emphasis, and the criteria of success. The resulting cultural typologies are: (a) clan cultures, (b) hierarchical cultures, (c) market cultures, and (d) adhocracy cultures. Clan cultures adhere to flexibility while focusing on the internal team. Hierarchical cultures focus on the internal team or organization but emphasize control and structure. Market cultures attention is on the external environment and how to use those parameters to adhere to control and structure. Finally, adhocracy cultures give control to the individual and emphasize creativity.

Clan Cultures

Clan cultures are based on a family dynamic where individuals feel that their roles are rooted in teamwork, and every individual is committed to the cause. Leaders tend to adhere to transformational or servant leadership styles, where they develop the employee to better the organization as a whole. The fundamental dynamics for the growth of this type of organization required openness, trust, and communication (Cameron & Quinn, 1999).

As the leadership cultivates the support of a work-family relationship with other team members, a clan culture work environment also helps individual employees. Through the support system, individuals find themselves taking the initiative and gaining confidence in their work and abilities. An employee who works in the clan culture typology has a sense of independence and is more inclined to feel safe and secure through the open environment the leadership creates.

However, due to the closeness and family atmosphere, this type of environment may exclude individuals who think in defense of the greater group and silence differing opinions and voices (Boogaard, 2022).

The most strenuous toxic traits of employees in the clan culture typology are self- promotion and unpredictability (Cameron & Quinn, 1999; Schmidt, 2008). In this type of workplace setting, a leader who self-promotes would inevitably combat the notion of a "family." In this case, they would make themselves greater than the group, which is the essential focus within the clan culture typology. If the leader portrays unpredictability, this destabilizes the consistency found in the clan culture. When people no longer know how their peers or leaders would react to a negative situation, the close ties and openness in the environment begin to break down (Schmidt, 2014).

Hierarchical Cultures

Structure and control promulgate hierarchical cultures. The environment is formalized through a strict set of rules that operates on the principle of bureaucracy. The leadership operates within a dictated pipeline and adheres to procedural systems that stem from institutional historical knowledge. In this environment, an organization is defined by predictability and consistency (Cameron & Quinn, 1999). To some employees, this provides a sense of safety in their work by disallowing the unknowns typical of more uneven or unstable typologies.

However, the slow chaos that stems from narcissistic and abusive leaders becomes far harder to recognize in this type of culture. Enron is an example where the mundane helped build toxicity in a self-perpetuating cycle. The hierarchical structure helped keep the toxicity from seeping beyond the confines of the organization by the public and employees' perception of consistency, and its leaders' narcissism disguised the toxicity as progress and success (Matos et al., 2018; McLean & Elkind, 2013).

In a hierarchical culture, an individual understands the role they fill, and the leadership plainly defines what is expected of them. Each person, from the lowest subordinate to the highest-ranking official, understands who they report to, who reports to them (if anyone), and what must occur in case of a breakdown in leadership. In other words, structure or procedural understandings are dictated and well defined (Boogaard, 2022; Cameron & Quinn, 1999). Due to the stringent nature of this type of work environment and the extreme adherence to command and control, a hierarchical typology leaves little room for individuals to express their own opinions and ideas. There is also no room to make self-directed decisions, as each decision point requires managerial oversight and is compartmentalized within the chain of command structure (RunMeetly, 2021).

A Hierarchical Cultural Example in Modern Corporate America

Enron is a perfect example of a hierarchical cultural typology gone astray. The senior executives at Enron demonstrated the toxic leadership traits of abusive supervision and narcissism (McLean & Elkind, 2013; Schmidt, 2008). The abusive supervision at Enron included taunting, public humiliation, and a system that terminated the bottom 10% of productive employees every year. This abusive supervision typically resulted in standing ovations for those fired or perceived to have failed, bullying from peers that escalated to physical abuse, and overall dissatisfaction among the majority. Although Enron is an extreme case of a toxic hierarchical culture, abusive supervision is allowed to fester in a compartmentalized entity with near-autonomous control from that entity's leadership (McLean & Elkind, 2013; Schmidt, 2008).

For someone to make it to the top of a hierarchical culture was an endeavor. Not all leaders portrayed narcissism, but in this type of culture, the trait was more prevalent. In the command structure of the hierarchical culture typology, the leader was the supreme being, and they rose to their position through their prowess (Schmidt, 2014). Finally, although not necessarily in the Enron case, the trait of authoritarianism is thought to likely have a greater effect on the organizational culture in a hierarchical typology. Micromanagement is common in leaders in a system that prides itself on process and method and shuns individuality and "outside- the-box" thinking. Employees and subordinates who enjoy the safe confines of this culture quickly lose the sense of security when the leadership turns toxic (Cameron & Quinn, 1999; Matos et al., 2018; Schmidt, 2014). The unsafe and unstable feeling of this change forces employees to look for ways to escape the toxic environment.

Market Cultures

In the market culture typology, results are a key factor in growth and prosperity. The entity looks externally at stakeholders like customers, clients, and even competitors for its guidance and benchmarks. The focus is goal-oriented, which demands tough and ruthless leaders to succeed. The main objective of this typology is to beat rivals at all costs and to aim for profitability (Cameron & Quinn, 1999). This culture is typical of banks and financial firms, such as Merril Lynch and Wells Fargo (Farrell, 2011; Ferrel & Ferrel, 2017), where the absence of control mechanisms and an aggressive sales force could overcome organizational policies and result in an extremely toxic environment.

The foundational principle of the market culture typology is to encourage an organization's competitive workplace, both internal and external (Boogaard, 2022; Cameron & Quinn, 1999). The goal is to experience rewards on a personal level, and leaders in this structure believe that if you reward an individual for their own merits and successes, the whole of the business unit and organization would thrive from those successes. The individual must succeed at any cost, and success at the business unit level influences and motivates other subordinates and business units to perform more aggressively (Boogaard, 2022). While leaders hope these individual successes motivate others to perform, this dynamic also tends to foster resentment, workplace exhaustion, and aggression. An inequitable reward system, enhanced and magnified by the public humiliation of perceived failure, has the potential to create an environment that promotes incivility (Johnson et al., 2016).

If the effects of a narcissistic leader continue without ramifications or oversight, the leader would continue to reap the greater team's benefits, portraying themselves as beacons of progress and self-promoting. In the end, the self-promoting leader never acknowledges their team's positive work and yet always places blame on the employees for any negative work. Those who are subordinate to narcissistic and self-promoting leaders in a market culture and exasperated from their perceived failures and unequal organizational justice inevitably harbor resentment for their employers and may begin to work against their employers' goals (Johnson et al., 2016).

A Market Culture Example in Modern Corporate America

The more prominent and detrimental toxic leadership traits in the market culture typology are narcissism, abusive supervision, and self-promotion. A leader chosen on the merits of their business acumen and ability to sell products only adheres to their sense of self (Ferrel & Ferrel, 2017). If the external environment deems an individual worthy of leadership due to the revenue they produce, that leader must be destined for great things (Schmidt, 2014). The narcissistic leader would ignore their subordinates' ideas, opinions, and work, ridiculing the ideas they perceive to be poor and stealing the ideas they perceive to be strong. Finally, a narcissistic leader always finds a way to win, even when sacrificing morals and ethics (Schmidt, 2014; Simmons, 2020). Eventually, when the work becomes unethical or illegal, the narcissist leader uses anyone near them as a scapegoat.

Wells Fargo Sales Pressure

In 2014, the immense sales pressure from Wells Fargo's market culture typology, which stemmed from the highest reaches of the company, forced the hand of the board of Wells Fargo via regulatory pressures. The aggressive and dangerous atmosphere that permeated from abusive senior executives created a self-perpetuating cycle that extended throughout the management (Irvine & Evans, 1995; Schmidt, 2014). The idea that a personal banker or customer service representative could lose their job for missing a sales quota for that quarter was not simply hearsay; it happened regularly (Ferrel & Ferrel, 2017).

Eventually, the practice of enforcing quotas forced the sales staff to choose between their careers and livelihoods and commit fraud at the customer's expense. Although some employees had the security of a safety net and were able to leave their roles, others chose to commit fraud out of fear of losing their jobs and the resulting financial hardships. For context, the fraud that took place involved opening both credit and personal banking accounts with the customers' consent, under pressure from the sales and branch managers. When the media and governmental agencies uncovered these practices, the individuals who committed fraud were fined, disbarred from the industry, and lost their licenses (Ferrel & Ferrel, 2017).

The toxic culture that forced the hands of its employees to choose between feeding their families through unethical and illegal means and getting fired was just one recent example of the many forms of toxic environments that stemmed directly from poor leadership (Boddy, 2013; Rupp, 2011; Tepper, 2000). In this study, I expand on the current research on the subject of toxic leadership and the cultures it created. I also affirm the relationship between the individual traits with each other, as well as turnover intention.

Adhocracy Cultures

The adhocracy typology of culture thrives on the entrepreneurial spirit and attempts to push boundaries through innovation and risk. Leaders want their subordinates to be self-motivated and energized while also being nimble, quick, and agile. This type of culture does well in the face of macro and micro change, and the leaders share a hands-off approach, giving their employees the freedom to maneuver and act on their ingenuity (Cameron & Quinn, 1999).

Employees who prefer autonomy and like challenges and the flexibility to respond to challenges with new ideas and ways of thinking enjoy this type of freedom (Boogaard, 2022; Down, 2019).

The adhocracy cultural typology thrives on employee individualism and innovation, with leaders who do not shame failure and applaud success. This culture relies on leaders to recognize defeat as a precursor to success and to coach their people to learn from the defeats and to keep moving forward. This type of leadership gains the most from out-of-the-box thinking (Boogaard, 2022). The downfall with this cultural typology is that it tends to obscure the delineations of power, leaving the roles and responsibilities unclear. The adhocracy typology may also blur the lines of effort about a company's current and future needs and goals. The flexibility and maneuverability of adhocracy cultures may prove faulty in more extreme cases as it replaces structure with flexibility. The lack of structure can be menacing during major economic downturns, internal organizational fallout, or office politics (Down, 2019).

The adhocracy cultural typology may have been permeated by the toxic leadership trait of unpredictability. An adhocracy culture relies on its flat-like structure concerning a lack of hierarchy and provides a backdrop for a potential leadership vacuum (Boogaard, 2022; Cameron & Quinn, 1999). In such cases of a leadership vacuum, combined with daily changes in a new company, the most aggressive individuals inevitably step in as stand-in managers or leaders. If the company is not doing well and successes are minimal, someone needs to take charge to try and right the ship. Either way, a culture already based on the interchangeability of the underlying structure feels more pronounced adverse effects from unpredictable and abusive leaders (Boogaard, 2022; Irvine & Evans, 1995; Schmidt, 2008). These leaders, who react without filter to both positive and negative situations, cause undue stress among the employees, who are already unsure of the organization's footing. This environment is more likely to produce subordinates who feel helpless, on edge, and unsafe (Schmidt, 2014).

Employees who operate successfully in an adhocracy environment do so because of the freedom it provides. An unpredictable leader takes away the employees' ability to operate freely and creatively due to personality extremes, specifically related to volatility (Down, 2019; Schmidt, 2014). The employee never truly knows what to expect on a minute-by-minute basis, which forces them to operate from within the confines of the leader's erratic and abusive behavior and stunts the creativity necessary for both the adhocracy culture and the employees to thrive (Boddy, 2013; Cameron & Quinn, 1999; Schmidt, 2008). This behavior leads employees to seek to leave the organization (Schlaegel et al., 2020).

Denison's Model

Very few competing theories are as well-known or utilized as the Competing Values Framework model. Cameron (2017) identified it as one of the most important business frameworks of all time, and it is currently used by over

12,000 companies worldwide (RunMeetly, 2021). Denison (2019), like Cameron and Quinn, found organizational cultures to use internal versus external traits with a range between control and flexibility. Denison found organizational cultures to have four basic elements: (a) consistency, (b) mission, (c) involvement/participation, and (d) adaptability. Consistency focuses on control and the internal team, and the idea is that this type of organizational culture is more in line with a community or family. The mission culture also focuses on control but is typically related to the external influencers that help the team toward collective goals. Involvement/participation looks internally at the foundation but remains flexible with changing environments. Finally, adaptability is both flexible and external and gives way to survival and growth (Denison, 2019).

Many other types of organizational cultures depend on specific situations or sectors. Organizational cultures have developed subgroups with social media and the internet, according to various business publications like *Forbes* and *Business Week*, and organizations like the Project Management Institute. However, none of these entities have produced scientific results that have changed how researchers categorize corporate cultures or typologies. This study used the framework of Cameron and Quinn (1999), following in the footsteps of dozens of other studies, and explored the toxic leadership traits in each of the four cultural typologies.

Job Satisfaction

In a toxic environment, the first collective problems appear in employee job satisfaction or dissatisfaction. Whether the employee loses motivation, disengages from their work and workplace, or is completely unsatisfied with their work, it manifests in their performance. Of course, a dissatisfied employee's tangible or fiscal cost can be great over time, and the intangible

costs are even higher (Bouchey & Glynn, 2012; Resick et al., 2013). A dissatisfied employee can help magnify the toxic environment, spread demoralization among other employees, cease or slow production, abruptly leave their role in hopes of a better environment, or counteract the team's efforts in ways that harm the overall organization (Leet, 2011).

Dissatisfied Employees' Performance

There is a direct link between job satisfaction and employee output and engagement. Job satisfaction can make or break an employee's assessment of their workplace and whether they intend to continue within their roles in the workplace. With job satisfaction, employees can visualize their future careers at the organization and are more inclined to work at their maximum capacity to progress (Seppalaa & Cameron, 2015; Tampubolon, 2016). However, dissatisfied employees tend to disengage and reevaluate their options and position in the organization (Leet, 2011). Tampubolon (2016) surveyed 90 employees in the import/export department of the Indonesian government and studied the relationship between employee engagement and job satisfaction. The study measured how job motivation, employee engagement, and satisfaction stemming from work affected the employees' performance. The results identified a clear feedback loop between the three variables, which ultimately enhanced employee performance.

When one of the variables was stressed, the other two also suffered (Irvine & Evans, 1995; Leet, 2011; Tampubolon, 2016).

In a nearly identical study in which Sudjiwanati and Pinastikasari (2020) focused on 171 participants with at least one year of full-time employment in Indonesia, the researchers found that an open communication environment had a positive impact on job satisfaction and employee engagement. The employees were able to communicate their needs and ideas openly to the management without fear of retribution or humiliation. In the same study, the researchers also

found that employee satisfaction and engagement positively influenced employee performance on both a professional and social level in the work environment (Sudjiwanati & Pinastikasari, 2020).

When employees begin to feel dissatisfied in their workplace because of a negative or toxic environment, they disengage from their work, which leads to performance issues.

Eventually, the spiral effect that stems from a toxic culture cultivated by a toxic leader combined with the stress of underperformance causes employees to leave their jobs (Bakkal et al., 2019).

Traits that Lead to Job Dissatisfaction

A Study on Emotional Intelligence and Leadership

In a 2020 study on 252 U.S. participants, 263 Indian participants, and 285 German participants, Schlaegel et al. (2020) attempted to link emotional intelligence to job satisfaction. Although there were slight differences among the countries and their need for emotional intelligence in their leaders, they all had significant statistical variances. The study concluded that a leader directly affects the subordinate's job satisfaction if the perceived emotional intelligence leadership traits of empathy, sympathy, listening, understanding, and openness are not present or actively utilized in the workplace (Schlaegel et al., 2020). The same researchers found that the leader's lack of emotional availability to the subordinate, or the disregard for emotional intelligence, had a negative impact on job satisfaction in all three countries, including the United States, Germany, and India.

Psychopathic Traits and Narcissism and Their Impact on Employee Engagement

Several studies have tested whether individual traits lead to employee dissatisfaction and disengagement. Boddy (2013) conducted a study in Britain and used a psychopathy scale in a direct management survey on 304 participants. Later, Boddy described perhaps the most extreme version of toxicity in a leader in a study on corporate psychopaths and the counterproductive output the typical employee displays in such unhealthy parameters. The researcher found that the psychopathic leader with no empathetic virtue who enjoyed emotional conflict was the largest contributor to workplace bullying, sabotage, and unethical decision-making (Boddy, 2013).

A 2020 study on 253 employees from nine different companies in China linked narcissism directly to employee disengagement, where leaders portrayed an unadulterated view of their self-worth and discarded that of their subordinates as inferior and inadequate (Chen et al., 2020). In both extremes of a toxic culture, the leader perpetuated negativity and further increased the likelihood of diminished productivity, employee disengagement, and dissatisfaction.

Linking Job Satisfaction to Turnover Intention

Bakkal et al. (2019) tested the perceptions of toxic leadership among healthcare employees in Turkey and the effects of this leadership on turnover intentions and job satisfaction. The results proved a statistical significance between job satisfaction and turnover intention, and the self-seeking trait significantly impacted job satisfaction. Upon the study's conclusion, Bakkal et al. suggested that every hospital in Turkey purge its management of toxic leaders or at least find ways to mitigate and cope with such behaviors. In an analytical review of three decades of studies among nurses in the United States, Irvine and Evans (1995) found that, while financial impact and personal conflicts did affect job satisfaction, the work environment in the cultural typology as promulgated through leadership has a stronger influence.

Incivility in the Workplace

Toxicity can also stem from a nonchalant leader who allows incivility to permeate by office politics. This type of leader displays the toxic leadership traits of unpredictability and abusive supervision (Schmidt, 2008). The office politics that stems from the employees themselves can turn negative with simple and subtle gestures, such as condescending comments, put-downs, and sarcasm (Johnson et al., 2016; Mawritz et al., 2012). The research by Johnson et al. on incivility in the workplace showed that this type of environment created an atmosphere of mental fatigue and diminished employee self-control, which led to further negativity in the workplace (Mawritz et al., 2012). The downward spiral that arose from a culture that self- perpetuated these seemingly minor gestures stemmed solely from the leaders. It was up to the leadership to create a healthy culture that limited such risk by enhancing decision-making practices and good governance (Stiroh, 2018; Tepper et al., 2004).

Toxicity and Turnover Intention

Common traits appear in the various studies on toxic leadership, such as abusive supervision and narcissism, but only one scientific paper used the entirety of Schmidt's (2008) validated toxic leadership scale. Leet (2011) conducted a study on 117 participants, over 65% based in Australia, while the remainder represented 25 other countries. Leet's study measured how a toxic or severely dysfunctional culture negatively affected an organization's production by focusing on employees' dissatisfaction and disengagement with the overall corporate output. The researcher found that toxic or severely dysfunctional leadership often led to turnover intentions, a loss of competencies or skills, higher costs to replace employees, disengagement, dissatisfaction, and a lack or total loss of motivation (Leet, 2011). The study sought to shed light on the output of a toxic culture and the intangible costs associated with this culture type to its employees and the organization.

Mediating Job Dissatisfaction

In "Toxic Leadership: The Most Menacing Form of Leadership," Singh et al. (2018) uncovered some nuances of toxic leadership, including specific traits, symptoms, and effects on an organization. The researchers' main focus was to shed light on the systemic issue of toxic leadership and open a dialogue within the corporate space. The researchers delineated the difference between toxic leaders, who selfishly used others for personal gain, and incompetent leaders who simply had poor managerial skills. They found that an environment that cultivates toxic attributes created stress, which led to counterproductive acts by the employees, including unethical and immoral acts. The stress from the environment manifested in the employees' both physical and emotional outputs and directly affected their work behavior, job satisfaction, morale, and, ultimately, turnover (Singh et al., 2018).

Typologies and Job Satisfaction

Organizational cultures or typologies like market culture, which perpetuates a more aggressive approach to conducting business, also tend to promote toxic leaders because of the focus on sales and production over internal management styles (Cameron & Quinn, 1999; Stiroh, 2018). A 2018 study on 1,000 U.S.-based participants focused on the abusive traits of male leaders and found harmful effects on the employees that extended well beyond the workplace (Matos et al., 2018). The data suggested that this type of leadership harmed the work/life balance, employee confidence, stress levels, job satisfaction, and turnover rates. The study proved that toxicity was harmful to the employee but also drew attention to a potential outlier concerning how certain men perceived toxic leaders even when they were negatively affected by them. The study suggested that some men perceive toxic leaders as something to aspire to.

Although they were negatively affected by these leaders, they still trusted their judgment and felt loyal to them. This study did not focus on gender roles in toxic environments, but these dynamics were collected and may be worth noting for future research.

Reed (2015) focused on the military and analyzed the toxic culture that plagued some of its most prominent senior leaders. Drawing on both public accounts of toxicity among these leaders and private accounts from active and retired troops, the data provided a backdrop for such leaders' long-term and potential career-ending effects. By studying the military, the truest form of the hierarchical culture typology (Cameron & Quinn, 1999), Reed encapsulated his version of a toxic culture via ego, pride, and a lack of humility and traced how these traits plague the prestigious U.S. Department of Defense. Junior troops who found themselves in a perceived toxic culture left life-long careers and suffered negative internal self-worth that outlasted their service. Due to the traits associated with this type of leadership, the civilian sector's organizational culture mimicked these leaders' traits and perpetuated the toxic environment (Boddy, 2013; Resick et al., 2013).

Healthy Leadership

The scientific literature on healthy or positive leadership is far more extensive and comprehensive than that on negative or toxic leadership. The key for a researcher of toxic leadership is to compare and contrast all the forms of leadership to derive the most succinct yet robust data supporting an overall conclusion or narrative. Regarding healthy leadership, subordinates prefer leaders who have direction, can decisively maneuver complicated or complex situations, and can motivate and influence not only their subordinates but the higher echelons of leadership as well. Subordinates require stability, the ability to grow within an organization, and having their immediate needs met (Hoppe, 2007).

Northouse (2013) conducted a multi-factor analysis of major studies on trait-centric positive leadership. The study suggested that positive traits like

(a) emotional stability, (b) openness, (c) social intelligence, (d) emotional intelligence, (e) sensitivity, and (f) trustworthiness were paramount to a well-adjusted and satisfied employee. The motivation and positive work environment the employees enjoyed allowed the company to be flexible in tough times and to take risks in periods of strength (Northouse, 2013).

A New Psychology of Leadership

Haslam et al. (2011) studied the new psychology of leadership, focusing on the new-age leader who both influences and creates a culture of positivity and affirming cultural identity. This new type of leader moves the group or unit in the same direction toward a common goal. Rather than pushing from behind or pulling from the front, a leader should act as the fulcrum and motivate their people to move in a collectively dictated direction (Haslam et al., 2011).

Much like servant leadership, the new-age leader cultivates every individual's talent and improves their weaknesses. Drawing on the employees' talents and weaknesses, a leader can help guide them by accessing and utilizing these traits. Servant leadership, which refers to a type of leader who leads by promoting the progress and wellbeing of their subordinates, helps motivate individuals. In so doing, the employees are poised for self-growth, which benefits the greater group and creates a positive influence (Savage-Austin & Honeycutt, 2011).

Emotional Intelligence and Good Leaders

The notion of positive leadership seems to derive from the connection between the leader and subordinate outside the confines of the employer's needs and mandates or the social contract between the employer and employee. Lindebaum and Cartwright (2010) examined 14 different U.K. construction companies with 227 participants. They found that emotional intelligence had a major role in the transformational leadership style and helped drive the connection between leaders and subordinates to not only create a positive and productive work environment but also spawn new leaders (Lindebaum & Cartwright, 2010).

A quasi-experimental study conducted in 2014 that focused on small unit teams in the U.S. Army introduced transformational leadership and trained the leaders of a poorly performing team. The study sought to verify whether or not transformational leadership could intercept a poorly performing entity at the unit level and improve performance through employee satisfaction and engagement. The study concluded that this emotionally based type of leadership style not only increased employee satisfaction and engagement but also helped ward off negative environmental factors through group cohesion and employee trust in the leadership (Arthur & Hardy, 2014).

Ethical Leadership

Morals and ethics also play a major role in positive leadership. In a study on the overall effects of a leader who displays strong moral and ethical standards, Resick et al. (2013) found that an ethical and moral attitude had a resounding effect on the overall culture. A leader who displayed a strong approach to right and wrong tended to help perpetuate the notion throughout the entirety of the entity, creating a safe and positive work environment. Comey (2018), a career Department of Justice executive-level leader, paid homage to such morals and ethics while offering insight on the positive traits he found to be the most beneficial among his subordinates: truth, objectivity, fairness, and humility. Comey found these traits to lend a hand in his subordinates' trust and willingness to make difficult decisions that may have been unpopular, but ethical and moral. The overall effect emulated a positive work environment.

The Benefit of a Positive Environment

Seppalaa and Cameron (2015) studied the positive aspects of leadership on an entire culture to prove or disprove the value of a positive approach in the growth and wellbeing of a company. This study was backed by quantitative data from the American Psychology Association and suggested that position within a hierarchical structure, disengagement, and a lack of loyalty could have costs for the employee, the employer, and even the U.S. economy. To avoid these risks, the researchers found that fostering social connection, displaying empathy, helping others (and oneself), and openness helped alleviate the various stressors in a negative environment to foster a healthy and preferred workplace (Seppalaa & Cameron, 2015).

The Scientific Emphasis on Positive Leadership

The emphasis on positive or prudent leadership in the scholarship shows that there is a real demand for strong leaders who treat people as individuals rather than as numbers and tools. Although there is also a great need to identify and thwart toxic leaders, the studies on ways to do so are limited. The reality was that the lack of attention to the negative side of leadership, or toxic leadership, was a lingering problem. Drawing on the extensive work by Schmidt (2008), who created a toxic leadership scale to help organizations identify toxicity within their ranks, I expanded on this knowledge. My study provides new insights that portray the strength of the relationship between toxic leadership traits defined by Schmidt (2008) and turnover intention.

Moreover, it addresses how individual traits affect turnover intention when modulated by the various cultural typologies provided by Cameron and Quinn (1999).

Healthy leadership has received enormous attention from the scientific community.

Discussions of healthy leadership offer a necessary contrast to those on toxic leadership and offer examples of what leaders should aspire to and how their positive influence can produce successful outcomes within any cultural typology. Therefore, to acquire an honest view of toxic leadership and its dangerous effects on any culture, we must discuss positive leadership first.

Turnover Intention

Turnover intention is the result of an extremely problematic corporate culture and environment. Although it does not always result from circumstances outside of the employee's control (e.g., wage loss, the inability to locate a similar role, fear of the unknown, health insurance loss), turnover intent is just as important (Roodt, 2013). Much like disengagement, disenfranchisement, and disloyalty, the turnover intention has consequences beyond the initial thought (Bouchey & Glynn, 2012). The worst-case scenario for a corporate entity is to lose an employee to a toxic environment, but several behaviors beyond toxic leadership can also eventually lead to the intent to leave the workplace.

Catalysts for Turnover Intention

Boddy (2013) was interested in the implications of corporate psychopaths, including who they are, how they operate, and what they mean for the overall organization. In addition to the traits associated with psychopathic management and leaders, specific organizational cultures like market cultures and hierarchical cultures (Cameron & Quinn, 1999) mimic the traits of these leaders and relay the toxic environment to their subordinates. The outcome of the study showed extenuating and significant impacts on organizational cultures, resulting in employee dissatisfaction and poor work performance.

Boddy's extensive work on negative corporate climate shows that these traits and this type of organizational behavior also impacted the employees' overall wellbeing. The problems of this culture went well beyond the work environment. Chen et al. (2020) linked narcissism to disengagement and argued that the narcissist trait had a significant negative effect on employees' ownership of their work and roles. The lack of ownership or control over their jobs led to disengagement (Chen et al., 2020).

A 2012 study on abusive supervision found that employee disengagement can be a catalyst for unethical and immoral acts among their peers, subordinates, and leaders (Mawritz et al., 2012). The team tested the trickle-down effects of an abusive manager on an abusive supervisor, with a moderator variable of the hostile work environment. The intent was to measure the overall effect on employees while combining the results with other international studies on abusive supervision to provide a comprehensive data set on the problem. The results showed that abusive supervision tended to trickle down to two levels of the hierarchy below the leader. In this way, toxicity permeated the culture and entire organization and provided the backdrop for ethical and moral dilemmas. It also perpetuated an environment that commonly used put-downs, sarcasm, and insults to motivate (Johnson et al., 2016).

The research showed that this type of environment bred mental fatigue and diminished employee self-control, leading to further workplace negativity and employee disenfranchisement. The employees also began to disassociate from their work to safeguard their mindset.

Corporate Scandals and Turnover

Disloyalty is another factor that stems from toxic leadership. Farrell (2011) wrote a well- researched history of Merrill Lynch that examined how the greed and ego of its leaders permeated the entire company and eventually led to its demise. The author focused on the toxic climate created by Stan O'Neil, the company's former CEO, and magnified through his top deputies. The insecurity and abusive supervision of the top leader at Merrill Lynch initially cultivated loyalty through fear but eventually led to employee burnout and disloyalty that fueled a mass exodus of talent and high turnover (Farrell, 2011).

Kenneth Lay, CEO of The Enron Corporation, similarly fueled a climate of ego, selfishness, and greed that led to the company's downfall. McLean and Elkind (2013), both renowned for their investigative journalism, provided valuable insight into the Enron Corporation's toxic environment. The writers exposed a senior leadership committee that enforced a 10% rule, which essentially removed the bottom 10% in productivity employees annually. Disloyalty festered as the sales team ignored morals, ethics, and their colleagues in a race to the bottom.

The characteristics that fester in toxic environments all eventually lead to the employees' turnover intentions. Roodt (2013) recognized that there were no reliable scales for the turnover intention that the community could use to analyze the fallouts of companies like Enron and Merrill Lynch and their hierarchical and market-driven cultural typologies (Cameron & Quinn, 1999). The study sought to compare the employees who left the companies and those who stayed to assess which variables in the organizations were the seemingly deciding factors. Considering that not all employees could simply leave their work environments, the researchers decided to look at the intention to leave a workplace rather than the actual act of leaving. The study investigated and compared turnover intentions, work-based identity scores, three dimensions of work engagement, three dimensions of burnout, organizational citizenship behavior, personal alienation, and task performance (Roodt, 2013).

The Costs of Turnover

There is a real cost of toxic leadership and cultures that self-perpetuate the tendencies of toxic leaders. Bouchey and Glynn (2012) reviewed 31 case studies on employee turnover from 11 of the most relevant research papers in an attempt to quantify the true cost of employee turnover. The associated costs were not only a detriment to the business but also the employee and the overall economic picture stemming from the American workforce and taxpayers. Approximately one-fifth of the total American workforce voluntarily leaves their job every year, costing roughly 20% of the $50,000 annual salary of an average or typical worker to replace that worker (Bouchey & Glynn, 2012).

The authors suggested that workplace policies that improve employee retention, like family-friendly policies, paid leave, and flexibility, can help companies reduce their turnover costs.

Sorenson and Garman (2013) discussed U.S. economic growth as a direct reflection of 70% of workers who are not working to their full potential. The study concluded that 52% out of the 70% of American workers who were not performing at their best were not engaged, and 18% of them were completely actively disengaged. The effect of not engaged or disengaged employees can cause "an emotional disconnect from their environment, possible working against their employers' interests, and they were less productive. These employees are also more likely to steal from their companies, negatively influence their coworkers, miss workdays, and drive customers away" (Sorenson & Garman, 2013, p. 2). Sorenson and Garman suggested several ways to combat this problem: employee engagement from the employer and leadership, selecting the right managers and training them to standard following defined principles, and finding ways to connect with employees.

Turnover intention is not the beginning of an employee's disengagement from their work and succumbing to the harmful emotions of an environment. Rather, it is the last destination of employees who can no longer work within the confines of the toxic environment (Bakkal et al., 2019). The research supplies data that turnover intention is the costliest symptom that stems from a toxic leader and the culture that permeates from them (Bouchey & Glynn, 2012; Jahn, 2020; McClear, 2019).

Organizational Justice

Organizational justice is part of the overall output of a toxic environment and extends beyond the individual employee. Organizational justice is defined as the perception of fairness within an organization. When employees feel safe, secure, and content within a work culture, there is a strong likelihood of positive job satisfaction and employee engagement (Rupp, 2011). Conversely, employees in cultures based on fear, abusive supervision, authoritarian leadership, narcissism, self-promotion, and unpredictability are less likely to be engaged and have no job satisfaction (Schmidt, 2008). The stronger the perception of organizational justice, the more difficult it is for such traits to thrive. A culture based on equity, openness, and trust helps protect a positive environment and detect the potential for a negative one (Northouse, 2013).

Types of Organizational Justice

Distributive Organizational Justice

Distributive organizational justice derives from equity, or the notion that resources are distributed equally, and any positive or negative reinforcement is disbursed fairly (Rupp, 2011). Distributive justice occurs in an organization that views its entire workforce as an asset and ensures employees receive the benefits of their labor fairly and without bias. In this type of organization, the introduction of traits of self-promotion and narcissism inhibits the leader's ability to distribute both praise and counseling equitably (Schmidt, 2008). A narcissistic leader who self-promotes only looks to boost those who inflate their self-image and severely shuns those who go against the grain or do not care to curtail their output for the leader's sake (Rupp, 2011; Schmidt, 2008; Simmons, 2020). A dangerous precedent takes hold through the self- perpetuating cycle of promoting those who best adhere to the leader versus those who do not.

Procedural Organizational Justice

Procedural organizational justice considers how leaders and the processes they use to make decisions are fair for all employees and are free of favoritism and bias (Rupp, 2011). The leader who portrays an authoritarian leadership style has the most to gain from controlling an organization's procedures (Rupp, 2011; Schmidt, 2014). Using their narcissism and self- promoting tendencies, an authoritarian leader can control an entire incentive and procedural process to ensure that those who show the highest loyalty receive the greatest gains (Colquitt, 2001; Rupp, 2011; Schmidt, 2008). The result shifts favor from those who are most capable and have the best ideas to those who simply bow down to the leader.

Informational Organizational Justice

Informational organizational justice focuses on both the openness and equal disbursement of information and how leaders use that information for explanatory purposes (Rupp, 2011). An authoritarian leader sees information as another form of control. In this instance, the authoritarian leader chooses the information they wish to divulge, creating an Orwellian-like environment that does not give the employees or subordinates the full picture they need to progress or succeed (Colquitt, 2001; Schmidt, 2008). Controlling the narrative through authoritative rule while adding the trait of unpredictability results in an extremely uncomfortable workplace where an individual is not only unsure of their stature within the organization but unsure of their worth and abilities (Rupp, 2011; Schmidt, 2014).

Interpersonal Organizational Justice

Interpersonal organizational justice involves how leaders treat their subordinates and the perception of that treatment among the organization about fairness (Rupp, 2011). A toxic leader's most menacing and personally dangerous trait, abusive supervision, plays a major role in workplace culture and affects interpersonal organizational justice (Schmidt, 2008; Singh et al., 2018). An employee or subordinate who endures a culture led by an abusive supervisor cannot fully function and produce. This type of leader controls their people through fear and forces loyalty and servitude through put-downs and negative feedback, no matter the ability or success of that employee (Schmidt, 2014).

Cultural Typologies and Organizational Justice

The cultural typology of an organization has a magnified effect on the overall perception of organizational justice. A clan culture may invite a family-type atmosphere, but as the company grows the team-oriented focus may become tribal with a decentralized award and discipline system, like an organization lacking distributive justice. Organizational justice may be equitable for a hierarchical typology, where a centralized system is strongest, and processes are maintained to a high degree. However, it may take humanity out of the final verdict in both positive and negative situations, creating a vacuum of information that affects the organization's interpersonal and informational organizational justice (Cameron & Quinn, 1999; Rupp, 2011).

A market typology tends to ignore equitable justice about distributive and interpersonal organizational justice, favoring those who produce over those who do not and harming the notion of equitable organizational justice.

Finally, adhocracy typologies may favor the most successful producers over those less productive but also emphasize those who take the greatest risks. When it comes to organizational justice, this typology may negatively affect the perception of procedural, distributive, and informational organizational justice, which inevitably affects the interpersonal organizational justice (Cameron & Quinn, 1999; Rupp, 2011).

Studies on Failed Organizational Justice

Ferrel and Ferrel (2017) conducted an expansive case study in which they looked at the extremes of a toxic environment, specifically at Wells Fargo and its latest attempts to rise from another scandal that involved not only fraud but also the toxicity of a sales-intensive workplace with a market-driven culture (Cameron & Quinn, 1999). This case study looked at the difference between the corporate responsibility aspect of Wells Fargo's "comeback plan," involving a community outreach initiative to give $444 million to over 11,000 charities in 2018, while the employees received a far more difficult comeback plan regarding their internal wellbeing within the company (Ferrel & Ferrel, 2017).

The study provided insight into Wells Fargo's external outreach program, which helped the local community but did not equate to a similar improvement in interpersonal or distributive organizational justice. The positive external outreach by Wells Fargo with no real improvement to their internal organizational justice severely harmed the wellbeing of the individual workers and subordinates (Rupp, 2011). The cultural typology of Wells Fargo, which is hierarchical and market-focused, provided the foundation for toxicity to permeate, trickle down, and become self- sustaining and cyclical (Mawritz et al., 2012).

Organizational Citizenship Behavior

In a 2004 U.S.-based study of 173 supervised employees, Tepper et al. (2004) found a relationship between the organizational behaviors of employees and the abusive supervision of leaders. Organizational citizenship behavior is comprised of job satisfaction and loyalty to an organization. The study found that when abusive supervision was displayed, the employees disengaged and became dissatisfied. The effects of this environment wreaked havoc on the organization, creating an unfair distribution of organizational justice and magnifying the leader's traits without further input from them (Tepper et al., 2004). The organization essentially became its source of toxicity, which the subordinates perpetuated. The study did not identify the type of culture or typology, but adhocracy cultures can mimic these types of results (Cameron & Quinn, 1999). Without a true leadership structure, an adhocracy can be overrun by the most successful player in the room. The rewards for that individual's success may be vastly greater than those for others' success, perpetuating unequal distributive justice and a toxic environment (Schmidt, 2014).

Combatting Organizational Injustice

Colquitt (2001) sought to deepen the understanding and perception of organizational justice to construct a validated scale of measurement. The researcher considered four types of organizational justice: procedural justice, distributive justice, interpersonal justice, and informational justice (Colquitt, 2001; Rupp, 2011). The work examined whether an organization was perceived as fair by employees regarding equality and openness in the workspace and, if not, how that unfairness related to job satisfaction, engagement, and production. Although the intent was to create a scale, Colquitt also proved that workers were either content or discontent in the workplace if they perceived the culture to be fair and believed justice was distributed without bias. The study thus showed that a toxic culture thwarts the idea of organizational justice, but it did not offer further information on whether organizational justice and the toxic environment change across the four different cultural typologies (Cameron & Quinn, 1999).

Stiroh (2018) looked at why employees can conduct potentially moral, ethical, or illegal acts that are contrary to the organization's stated principles to achieve an underlying corporate goal. The author suggested that these heinous acts are not simply the product of a few individuals but stem from a major breakdown in the organizational culture. Stiroh looked at "cultural capital" as the key to reducing that risk. The greater the cultural capital, or the closer a company is to guiding their organization to the stated corporate initiatives and values, the better the company is at self-correcting and reducing the risk of bad actors. Stiroh suggested that to combat the blatant toxicity that permeated sales-associated environments, the leadership is responsible for creating a healthy culture that limits risk by enhancing decision-making practices and "good governance" (Stiroh, 2018).

Summary

There is an abundance of well-researched information on the topic of leadership. When it comes to the scientific data-driven literature on leadership, studies usually focus on positive leadership in the attempt to help HRM identify what is expected in modern-day leaders. There is, in fact, no singular definition of what a perfect leader is, especially when each cultural typology seems to prefer a different group of traits to enhance the organization's underlying structure.

Finally, by using only the positive traits, HRM is more likely to find the same positives that have reverberated throughout the individual leader's career. Therefore, when a leader is chosen because of their positive traits, the decision is based purely on their success in the environment or typology they managed, while the new organization does not know that environment and only sees the positive attributes they bring to the table.

While there is a good amount of information on toxic leadership, much of it stems from after-the-fact or past-tense discoveries. The data-driven literature on toxic leadership is scattered, seldomly quantifiable, and does not offer the necessary blueprint for HRM to identify the less- visible harmful traits of leaders. The literature clearly shows which traits are negative and what obstacles they lead to. However, the hierarchy of which traits are better or worse and how these affect each typology is less clear. I addressed these problems and answered some of the lingering questions in the current literature.

This chapter discussed toxic leadership, cultural typologies, job satisfaction, healthy leadership, turnover intention, and organizational justice. Using Schmidt (2008) and the Shortened Version Toxic Leadership Scale, Cameron and Quinn (1999) and their Competing Values Framework, and Roodt's (2013) Turnover Intention Scale, I looked to deepen the discussion on toxic leadership in the current literature. The next chapter discusses the study methodology.

Chapter 3: Methodology

The purpose of this quantitative cross-sectional non-experimental study was to determine if relationships existed between certain toxic leadership traits (i.e., the independent variable or IV) and employee turnover intentions (i.e., the dependent variable or DV) and if those relationships were different across various organizational culture typologies (i.e., the moderating variable or MV). Findings from prior studies on toxic leadership (Chen et al., 2020; Matos et al., 2018; Mawritz et al., 2012; Schmidt, 2014) have focused on either singular traits and their effects on employees or the overall effects of toxic leadership on an organization's culture.

I have chosen the quantitative research method for this study to use the sample population to make generalizations about the overall population (Albers, 2017). The parameters of the study were based on individuals in the United States who had worked full-time in their current roles for at least one year, were subordinate to another individual (i.e., a leader), did not work at an executive level (i.e., C-suite) capacity, and identified themselves as working within one of the four cultural typologies defined by Cameron and Quinn (1999).

Research Method

There was a gap in the current literature on ways to adequately evaluate toxic leadership traits in different workplace cultures. This study looked to determine the relationship, and strength of the relationship, between the five toxic leadership traits Schmidt (2008) associated with turnover intentions. Those relationships were tested within the four cultural typologies of Cameron and Quinn (1999), attempting to see if there were changes in the strengths of the relationship and the influence within the cultural typologies. I aimed to add to the research on the nature of and degree that different toxic leadership traits might influence employee performance and turnover intentions within different cultural typologies.

Procedure and Participant Selection

I used Momentive (formally SurveyMonkey) to create and disseminate the digital survey and collect participants' data. After collecting the data, I used Momentive to format it in an ingestible version of the SPSS ® Software for analysis (Gligor et al., 2013; IBM, 2022).

Momentive is a popular and reliable web-based survey platform that allows a researcher to design, create, and conduct surveys. Momentive also has an extensive online database with a "Consumer Panel" and "Audience" application that gives researchers access to millions of people around the world (Gligor et al., 2013; Momentive, 2021). I used Momentive due to its ease and accessibility and ability to formulate data for analytical purposes (Momentive, 2021).

Access to Momentive's "Consumer Panel" allows for easier data collection while protecting the participants' identities (Gligor et al., 2013). Momentive's "Audience" application gives researchers access to the desired participants by pre-screening potential participants via specific and targeted attributes before disseminating the survey (Momentive, 2021). The prescreening occurred before participants had access to the study, and I also screened within the survey to ensure the standards were met. The participants were asked to verify five qualifiers or criteria before the questionnaire was available to them:

They were 18 years of age or older. To proceed to the survey questionnaire, the participant had to affirm "yes" to this criterion. Although this study did not examine age as a variable, this qualifier was necessary for the researcher to ascertain that the potential participant was of legal age in the United States.

They were citizens or residents of the United States and worked in a U.S.-based organization. To proceed to the survey questionnaire, the participants were asked to affirm "yes" to the criterion. This qualifier was necessary to ensure the study was restricted to American employees in organizations based in the United States.

They were currently employed full-time. To proceed to the survey questionnaire, the participant had to affirm "yes" to this criterion. This qualifier determined participant eligibility within the parameters set by this researcher.

They were employed with their current employer in their current role for at least one year. To proceed to the survey questionnaire, the participants had to affirm "yes" to this criterion. This qualifier determined participant eligibility within the parameters set by this researcher.

Their current position was not an executive leadership (C-suite) role. To proceed to the survey questionnaire, the participant had to affirm "yes" to this criterion. This qualifier determined that participants are subordinate in nature and report to at least one person of higher authority.

I acknowledge that C-suite employees may report to a Chief Executive Officer (CEO) or that the CEO may report to a Board of Directors or Trustees. However, the intent was to survey participants who held director-level positions or worked at lower ranks and may have less influence throughout the entire organization.

I gathered demographic information but did not use it for analytical purposes in this study. It is only for informational purposes and may become the focus of future studies. The first section consisted of typical demographic questions, including questions on sex, ethnicity, type of work (e.g., non-profit, for-profit, governmental, or military), the total length of time working at their job, and a question on time spent working during the COVID-19 pandemic. Responses to these non-identifiable questions were used to determine if participants were representative of the general population after data collection was completed. External of Momentive's process to gather demographical data, I included the same demographic questions I discussed previously in the survey. The program matched participants' demographic data with those who completed the questionnaire, ensuring that everyone who completed the survey had access to the information. Momentive assigned a number to the surveys to ensure the participants' anonymity and to compare and analyze the responses (Momentive, 2021).

Informed Consent Form

Using Momentive's digital platform, I created an informed consent form to ensure the participants had a thorough understanding of the nature of the survey, the procedures of administering and completing the survey, and how I used Momentive's Application to obtain the data. The informed consent form ensured the participants understood their right to opt out of participating in the survey at any time and informed them of how Momentive and I protected their data (Momentive, 2021). In the text of the informed consent form, I removed language that may have influenced participants' responses to mitigate unintended bias. As a result, the form referred to leadership traits without using the word "toxic" and to employee intentions without using the word "turnover." By keeping the language in the form neutral and omitting certain words, the questions themselves should have had little to no effect on the truthfulness of the participants' responses.

The informed consent form also notified the participants that they were not to be paid for their participation but that their involvement would add value to the study. The informed consent form provided them with my contact information in case they had questions or concerns. The informed consent form ensured the participants were informed of possible risks and discomfort, which would be minimal, associated with completing the survey and mitigating steps they could take. The consent form also alluded to the mandatory attributes the study required, such as the participant being over 18 years of age, U.S. residents who worked in U.S.-based organizations, not employed in executive-level positions, and qualified to participate in the study. By submitting the consent form to Momentive via a radial button, the participant affirmed they met the qualifications for this study and moved on to the next portion of the survey.

The Survey

After agreeing to the consent form, the participant moved on to the survey questionnaire, which consisted of four main sections. The first section was one page long and requested the participants to answer five demographic questions and one question regarding their time at work due to the COVID-19 pandemic. The question regarding the amount of time spent working from home due to the COVID-19 pandemic was in direct response to the abnormal reality of the COVID-19 pandemic. The expectation was that a larger number of participants set by this researcher would be working from home or other remote locations due to the prevailing health emergency but may still be subject to toxic leadership.

Keeping the pandemic in mind, I had to recognize and account for the abnormal and special circumstances. The study did not directly analyze the effects of remote work on toxicity or turnover intentions, but I intended to have an idea of the possible influences of these dynamics on the participants' responses and the possible limitations of my research. Those effects may be worth researching in the future. This question did not return reliable results and was discarded from the analysis.

In the next section, the participants responded to a single prompt based on Cameron and Quinn's (1999) four organizational culture typologies to self-identify their workplace typology. Participants chose the typology description defined by Cameron and Quinn (1999) that best described their current workplace. The descriptions were not identified as "clan," "hierarchy," "market," or "adhocracy" to avoid confusing the participants and/or creating bias, as certain labels may have influenced the participants' responses. The descriptions were dummy coded as the following: "Workplace 1 (WP 1)," which stood in for "clan" typology; "Workplace 2 (WP 2)," which stood in for "hierarchical" typology; "Workplace 3 (WP 3)," which stood in for "market" typology; and "Workplace 4 (WP 4)," which stood in for "adhocracy" typology (Cameron & Quinn, 1999).

The validated instrument Cameron and Quinn (1999) created, the Organizational Culture Assessment Instrument (OCAI), allowed the users to identify their current workplace typology and later choose the typology they perceived to be best suited for them. Users must plot scores by numerical points ranging from 1 to 100, evaluating four dimensions of the typologies that corresponded with each of the researchers' Cultural Values Framework. I decided against using this instrument as it was intended for higher-level managers in organizational change initiatives; therefore, I did not believe it was appropriate for this study. Lower-level leaders, or leaders in general, may not be familiar with the science of organizational studies and may not be able to estimate the degree or percentage to which the different dimensions existed. Instead, I chose to present the definitions used for the four different cultural typologies as defined by Cameron and Quinn (1999) so that the participants in this study would have a more reasonable understanding of the nature of their workplaces and could more easily identify their typology.

The third section of the survey questionnaire included the validated Shortened Toxic Leadership Scale from Schmidt (2008). The final section of the survey used the validated abbreviated Turnover Intention Scale or TIS-6 from Roodt (2013). These sections were a total of three pages long. Pages one and two tested toxic leadership using the shortened version of the Toxic Leadership Scale (Schmidt, 2008), while page three included the TIS-6 (Roodt, 2013) to measure employee turnover intentions.

Instruments

Schmidt's Toxic Leadership Scale

Schmidt (2008) recognized the media's emphasis on toxic leadership but realized there was little scientific study on the subject. When the researcher began to research the phenomenon, the traits other researchers had used to describe toxic or dysfunctional leadership varied and were not uniform, and there was no formal scale of measurement. Schmidt used the most cited articles of the time to compile a list of traits to describe toxic leadership and then tested them in a multidimensional study. The first part of the study defined and codified themes through focus groups and interviews with 23 U.S. military personnel. The second part of the study took the traits derived from the qualitative themes and tested them in a questionnaire format on 218 undergraduate students from a large mid-Atlantic university (Schmidt, 2008).

Schmidt (2008) used the findings to create a validated scale of measurement by identifying and ranking the themes and producing the top five traits associated with toxic leadership. Schmidt (2008) and the Toxic Leadership Scale tested the employees' perception of toxic leadership via the five common toxic traits he identified: (a) abusive supervision, (b) narcissism, (c) unpredictability, (d) self-promotion, and (e) authoritative leadership.

Schmidt (2008) also introduced a validated shortened version of the Toxic Leadership Scale with a total of 15 items. The shortened version achieved the same or similar outcomes as the original scale. To lessen the burden of completing the original scale on the participants, maximize the participation rate, and maintain the quality of responses, I chose to use Schmidt's shortened version of the Toxic Leadership Scale (Momentive, 2021; Sahlqvist et al., 2011). I used it to validate whether the participant was actively working under toxic leadership and to measure the toxic traits concerning culture typology. This validated scale of measurement appeared as the first scale in the survey questionnaire. Dr. Paul J. Hanges granted me approval to use the scale. Dr. Hanges mentored Schmidt during his graduate studies at the University of Maryland when Schmidt created the Toxic Leadership Scale, and he has the authority to grant permission on Schmidt's behalf.

Cronbach's alpha reliability scale measured the reliability rating of each of the five toxic leadership traits on the shortened scale. Created to measure the internal consistency, or interrelatedness, of a scale of measurement, it is expressed as a number between 0 and 1 (Tavakol & Dennick, 2021). A Cronbach's alpha measurement above 0.80 is considered valid. The results from testing Schmidt's Toxic Leadership Scale with the Cronbach's alpha scale are as follows: abusive supervision: α=0.93, authoritarian leadership: α=0.89, narcissism: α=0.88, self-promotion: α=0.91, unpredictable leadership: α=0.92. The Toxic Leadership Scale is measured using a 6-point Likert scale, with 1 representing "Strongly Disagree" and 6 representing "Strongly Agree."

Roodt's Turnover Intention Scale (TIS-6)

The study also tested turnover intentions using the Roodt (2013) Turnover Intention Scale (TIS-6), which appeared as the second scale in the survey questionnaire (see Appendix B).

Roodt's (2013) Turnover Intention Scale is a validated scale that considers an employee's work engagement, work-based identity, burnout, helping behaviors, work alienation, and task performance. Roodt (2013) understood that the ability to leave a role depended on many factors outside of the work situation; they subsequently introduced a scale related to the employee's intent to leave a role or position. The decision to use the validated shortened version of the TIS-6 was once again to limit the burden on participants and to maximize the participation rate and quality of responses (Momentive, 2021; Roodt, 2013; Sahlqvist et al., 2011). The shortened version achieves the same or similar outcomes as the original scale.

The final page of the questionnaire contained the six-item survey. Employee turnover intention aims to effectively measure the perceived severity of the leadership traits and the participants' intention to leave their organizations. The baseline of this measurement was the employee's perception of the ability to leave their role for a similar job, as influenced by the organizational cultural typology that best described the participant. This baseline determined if the participants intended to leave their organizations due to toxic cultures that stemmed from leadership behaviors. Roodt, who created the original and modified Turnover Intention Scale, granted me approval to use the scale.

Roodt (2004) published the first version of the Turnover Intention Scale, which had a Cronbach's alpha coefficient of α=0.913 and originally had a total of 15 items. Roodt (2013) later published a shortened version of the scale, known as TIS-6, which included six items from the 15-item scale. The TIS-6 has a Cronbach's alpha coefficient of α=0.80. The two-tailed Pearson coefficient analyzed the answers of respondents who remained at the company (M=4.13, SD=1.28) versus those who left (M=5.14, SD=1.26). The difference in the means had a significant effect (η2/p=0.14), proving that the TIS-6 was a reliable predictor of turnover intention and could decipher between those who stay and those who leave (Roodt, 2013). The Roodt (2013) Turnover Intention Scale uses a 5-point Likert scale.

Power Analysis

I used *a priori* analysis with G Power version 3.1.9.7 to calculate the sample size versus power for the study with a significance level of 0.05 and a power of 95% (Faul et al., 2007). The calculation did include linear regression, with six predictors for analysis. The standard deviation for the power level is 0.80, with a probability level of α=0.05. This formula determined that this study's minimum number of surveys would be *n*=146. For this study, I was able to capture a total of 613 (n=613) participants. A medium effect size of 0.50 is the threshold to ensure the strength of the relationships between variables is not overly strict or lenient (Faul et al., 2007). I used a combination of linear and categorical analysis to correlate the variables.

Population and Sample

Population

The appropriate population is key to obtaining the most accurate data for analysis. I have evaluated adult American workers' perceptions of toxicity within their current workplaces and their intent to leave their organizations due to negative work environments caused by toxic leadership. Due to the current COVID-19 pandemic, I also considered the effects of the pandemic on the traditional American work-life and have accepted participants who work virtually. However, as the impact on participants may change due to the space created by physical distance from toxic leaders, this accommodation may have influenced the data. The importance of the population was to fully understand the perceptions of regular, full-time workers in the United States to gain the best insight into the proposed phenomena (Hoe & Hoare, 2013).

As for gender, race, ethnicity, and levels of education and experience, I attempted to have a participant sample that represented the demographics of today's society. I captured the data in the demographic section of the survey, but I did not use demographic data for analytical purposes in this study. The information obtained may be used for future studies. The assumption was that employees from different demographics related to toxicity and job satisfaction differently, but
the composite of every corporate environment would vary based on its geographic locality. The intent was to survey participants from across the United States. Therefore, allowing data collection in the form of a simplified random sampling has strengthened the results (Marshall & Batten, 2004).

Sample

I utilized the extensive network built into Momentive's database to most efficiently and effectively screen for the desired participants and identify a sample size to accurately depict the greater population (Gligor et al., 2013; Momentive, 2021). The study focus was on American workers who have been employed in their current position at a U.S.-based workplace for one year or more and who may or may not perceive to be operating in a toxic environment. Although the data was captured, there was no delineation between employees who work in the public (e.g., governmental workers), private sectors (e.g., corporations), or the military. The reason for not emphasizing industries or sectors was to focus more on workplace culture, as described by Cameron and Quinn's (1999) typologies. The minimum size for this study was 148, with a target of an even distribution of population size (0.25) per the four cultural typologies, for a total of 37 participants per typology.

Ensuring the Sample Is Met

The minimum number of 37 participants was met for each typology. To achieve the threshold, I had to launch the survey two times as the initial launch on

January 18, 2022, and completed on January 19, 2022, did not satisfy the minimum requirements for complete data collection. The second launch began and ended on February 4, 2022, and captured more responses than expected, exceeding the minimum threshold. The participants answered all the questions to complete the survey and clicked the "submit" button. Momentive discarded any incomplete surveys. There was a greater number of participants from some typologies than others, which was anticipated. The final achieved sample size was a total of 613 participants.

The participant breakdown per culture typology had 235 identified as working within a clan-culture typology and 235 as working within a hierarchical-culture typology. A total of 84 identified as working in market culture, and 59 identified as working in an adhocracy-culture typology. In analyzing the data for all four cultural typologies, I acknowledge that participants who worked in some typologies might have yielded more robust data because of the larger number of participants who identified as working within those typologies.

Data Analysis

The data from the survey questionnaire was input from Momentive to the SPSS ® Software for data analysis (Momentive, 2021; Selya et al., 2012). To test both the correlation and strength between variables, I analyzed possible correlations between the individual toxic leadership traits Schmidt (2008) identified as (a) abusive supervision, (b) narcissism, (c) authoritative leadership, (d) self-promotion, and (e) unpredictability, and employee turnover intentions as measured with the TIS-6 (Roodt, 2013). Using the General Linear Model, I examined whether the predictors (i.e., toxic leadership traits) influenced the outcome (i.e., turnover intention), with the addition of culture typology as a moderating variable, to identify correlations.

Next, to test the correlation between the independent and dependent variables to verify the data, I completed a Bivariate Correlation to identify the strength between each toxic leadership trait within the Toxic Leadership Scale (Schmidt, 2014) while including turnover intention. Using the Pearson 2-tailed correlation, I wanted to see if there was a significant correlation between every toxic leadership trait and turnover intention.

I analyzed whether there is a relationship between the individual toxic leadership traits Schmidt (2008) identified—(a) abusive supervision, (b) narcissism, (c) authoritative leadership, (d) self-promotion, and (e) unpredictability—and employee turnover intentions as noted in TIS-6 (Roodt, 2013). Using multiple linear regression analysis, I examined whether the predictors (toxic leadership traits) affect the outcome (i.e., turnover intention).

Afterward, I tested the outcome of the relationship between the IV (i.e., toxic leadership traits) and DV (i.e., turnover intention) by introducing the MV (i.e., culture typology) using a 2- way Univariate Model. I analyzed the relationship between each trait and turnover intention, the relationship strength, and changes in those relationships by adding a cultural typology.

Finally, I used a Post Hoc Test to measure the relationship between workplace typology and turnover intention. I broke out the four Workplace Typologies to further analyze the individual relationships between each workplace and Turnover Intention. The intent was to see if the four various workplaces also had a significant effect on turnover intention.

Ethical Assurances

With this focus on human behavior in the workplace, I was mindful of several key factors to operate ethically. Because the research was meant to aid HRM in professional development related to organizational leadership, the population also included "vulnerable individuals," which possibly increased the potential for ethical or moral issues during the period of research (Koocher, 2013). This study ensured the maximum care and protection of the individuals who chose to participate. As with all psychological research, the study attempted to promote human welfare in a corporate setting. I was dedicated to not only benevolent actions but also the greater notion of the betterment of society. It is important that the information was accurate, the study was conducted in a way appropriate for a psychological professional and moves society forward to better the world and improve the lives of fellow humans (Koocher, 2013; Marshall & Batten, 2004).

I preserved the collected information digitally on a secure and encrypted site. I maintained my data analysis in the encrypted cloud, and the results have concealed any personally identifiable information (Gligor et al., 2013). Aside from the security of the information, the conduct towards participants was also essential. The survey was simple, easy to read, non-pretentious, and culturally sensitive (Marshall & Batten, 2004). The views expressed by the participant may have an impact on society as I sought to find more effective ways for humans to grow and prosper based on different people's psychological and emotional needs. For this reason, I took extra precautions to ensure participants' emotional and psychological wellbeing. My overall goal was to give back to society through academic and scientific means without creating further stressors for the very people we serve (American Psychological Association, 2017).

Before administering the survey, a consent form presented the participants with a detailed outline of the steps to be taken to secure their information and protect their identity. As per the consent form, participants were able to elect not to participate, and/or they could stop the survey at any time. The consent form also stated that the purpose of the study was for data collection in an academic research study. The information was not for sale or accessible to any other individual or organization. Finally, the consent form included my personal contact information for future correspondence.

Validity

Mitigating errors were often the most important element when considering not only the structure of the survey but also the outcome and analysis. I have thus taken care to determine the survey's scope, the methods used to create and conduct the survey, and to ensure that any practitioner bias was eliminated with every question. The questionnaire was written to be as unbiased and neutral as possible, with special attention to wording that could elicit emotional responses and skew the participants' answers (Momentive, 2021).

Other major obstacles included social desirability and conformity bias, considering the delicate nature of accurate responses and the real effects they may have on the participants' livelihoods. When attempting to define toxicity and what toxic leadership means to non- managerial workers, I was cognizant of posing questions that might drive a socially acceptable response external to truth or invoke "group norm" thinking that may potentially skew the participant chosen answers (Momentive, 2021). The survey avoided language that led participants to provide "socially desirable" answers or "conformity" and "neutrality" response bias (Burchett & Ben-Porath, 2019). The survey and the written consent form attempted to avoid these biases by ensuring information was randomized, kept confidential, and protected.

Summary

This chapter provided an overview of the potential research methodology and procedures. It discussed the informed consent form and expanded on privacy concerns, the intentions for the data use, and the survey flow. It also described the survey in detail, along with how I intend to use the Toxic Leadership Scale outlined by Schmidt (2008) and the TIS-6 from Roodt (2013). It also identified the population, specific sample description, and the reasoning for using Momentive. Finally, I discussed the data analysis procedures, ethical considerations, and validity. The next chapter presents the data from the study.

Chapter 4: Data Analysis and Results

The purpose of this quantitative, cross-sectional, non-experimental study was to determine if relationships exist between toxic leadership traits and employee turnover intentions among participants working in one of four organizational culture typologies. Using Schmidt's (2008) Toxic Leadership scale, Roodt's (2013) Turnover Intention Scale, and a singular question referencing the four culture typologies of Cameron and Quinn's (1999) Competing Values Framework, I collected quantifiable data examining the relationships between the three variables. The data collection began on January 18, 2022, and ended on February 6, 2022. The study was conducted on Momentive's platform utilizing Momentive's Audience application, a market research application that helps recruit random participants. Chapter 4 provides the quantitative analysis of the study.

Data Analysis

Using the G-Power analysis, the minimum number of participants required for this study was 146 (N=146), with a minimum of 37 participants per typology. As illustrated in Table 1, a total of 613 participants responded to each question of the study providing a more accurate depiction with a smaller margin of error (Faul et al., 2007). The study included a cross-section of 665 respondents, of whom 627 qualified to participate in the study. Of the 627 participants who answered the initial five demographical questions, 613 completed the full survey.

First, I decoded the workplaces to parse the data from the study. Workplace 1 is identified as the Clan-culture typology; Workplace 2 is identified as the Hierarchical-culture typology; Workplace 3 is identified as the Market-culture typology; Workplace 4 is identified as the Adhocracy-culture typology (Cameron & Quinn, 1999).

Out of these 613 qualifying participants, 235 identified as working within a Clan-culture typology (i.e., Workplace 1); 235 identified as working within a Hierarchical-culture typology (i.e., Workplace 2); 84 identified as working in a Market-culture typology (i.e., Workplace 3); and 59 identified as working in Adhocracy-culture typology (i.e., Workplace 4), typologies identified by Cameron and Quinn (1999). Please see Table 1 for these findings.

Table 1: Workplace Type

Answer Choices	Percentage	Numerical
Workplace (WP) 1	38.34%	235
Workplace (WP) 2	38.34%	235
Workplace (WP) 3	13.70%	84
Workplace (WP) 4	9.62%	59
Total	100.00%	613

Demographics

Gender. I collected 627 total responses with five questions regarding demographics. Table 2 provides the visual breakdown of the gender of each participant. As a footnote, the demographical information was not used in the final analysis as it serves as a foundation for future research. Out of the 627 total responses to the gender demographic question, 58.69% identified as female, 39.55% identified as male, 0.64% identified as non-binary, 0.16% identified as transgender, 0.32% identified as intersex, and 0.64% chose to type in their responses by accessing the "Let me type..." function. Out of the four participants who chose to write in their answer for "gender," one individual wrote "Agender," and the three others avoided the question with non-topical feedback on the subject.

Table 2: Gender

Answer Choices	Percentage	Numerical
Female	58.69%	368
Male	39.55%	248
Non-binary	0.64%	4
Transgender	0.16%	1
Intersex	0.32%	2
Let me type.	0.64%	4
Total	100.00%	627

Ethnicity. Table 3 provides information on the 627 participants who answered the Ethnicity demographic question, with 1.44% identified as "none of the above." A total of 11.64% identified as "Asian or Pacific Islander," 7.34% identified as "Black or African-American," 8.61% identified as "Hispanic or Latino," 1.28% identified as "Native American or Alaskan Native," and 2.39% identified as "Multi or Biracial." Finally, the majority of respondents, 67.3%, identified as "White or Caucasian."

Table 3: Ethnicity

Answer Choices	Percentage	Numerical
None of the above	1.44%	9
Asian or Pacific Islander	11.64%	73
Black or African- American	7.34%	46
Hispanic or Latino	8.61%	54
Native American or Alaskan Native	1.28%	8
White or Caucasian	67.30%	422
Multiracial or Biracial	2.39%	15
Total	100.0%	627

Type of Job. The Type of Job demographic question within the study allowed for a multiple-choice option. The multiple-choice option allowed a single participant to input multiple job types for their current job, which increased the responses but still maintained the number of 627 participants. In Table 4, 627 participants responded a total of 647 times, which resulted in

103.19% of responses and skewed the data. In my study and analysis, I did not take into consideration this demographic, so the problems with the data do not affect my overall findings. Out of that inflated total, 6.54% identified as a Federal Governmental Worker. A total of 16.91% identified as working for a Non-Profit organization, and 49.44% identified as working for a For- Profit Organization. A total of 1.75% identified as working as a member of the Military, and 28.55% identified as working in "Other."

Table 4: Type of Job

Answer Choices	Percentage	Numerical
Federal Government Worker	6.54%	41
Non-Profit	16.9%	106
For-Profit	49.4%	310
Military	1.75%	11
Other	28.5%	179
Total	103.19%	647

Length of Time at Current Job. In Table 5, of the 627 participants who answered the Length of Time at Current Job demographical question, 18.82% identified as working at their job between 12-18 months. A total of 17.7% responded as working at their job between 18-36 months, and 13.24% responded as working at their job between 36-60 months. Finally, 50.24% responded with working at their current jobs for 60 or more months.

Table 5: Length of Time at Current Job

Answer Choices	Percentage	Numerical
12-18 Months	18.82%	118
18-36 Months	17.70%	111
36-60 Months	13.24%	83
60 Months or More	50.24%	315
Total	100.00%	627

Education Level. In Table 6, of the 627 participants who answered the Educational Level demographic question, 10.69% identified as completing high school. A total of 22.65% identified as having "Some College," 33.81% identified as completing a "Bachelor's Degree," and 6.54% identified as having completed "Some Master's Level Work." Additionally, 15.79% identified as having "Completed Master's Degree," 1.91% completed "Some Doctoral Level Work," 3.67% identified as having "Completed a Doctorate," and finally, 4.94% identified as having completed "Technical/Trade College."

Table 6: Education Level

Answer Choices	Percentage	Numerical
High School	10.69%	67
Some College	22.65%	142
Completed Bachelor's Degree	33.81%	212
Some Master's Level Work	6.54%	41
Completed Master's Degree	15.79%	99
Some Doctoral Level Work	1.91%	12
Completed Doctorate	3.67%	23
Technical/Trade College	4.94%	31
Total	100.00%	627

Toxic Traits Influence on Turnover Intention and Culture Typology

General Linear Model with Each Toxic Leadership Trait

The data from the survey questionnaire was input into SPSS® Software for data analysis (Selya et al., 2012). First, I analyzed possible correlations between the individual toxic leadership traits Schmidt (2008) identified as (a) abusive supervision, (b) narcissism, (c) authoritative leadership, (d) self-promotion, and (e) unpredictability, and employee turnover intentions as measured with the TIS-6 (Roodt, 2013). Using the General Linear Model, I examined whether the predictors (i.e., toxic leadership traits) influenced the outcome (i.e., turnover intention), with the addition of culture typology as a moderating variable, to identify correlations.

The statistics presented in Table 7 reveal that the only significant (p= <.05) influence over turnover intention is the workplaces (p=<.001). These results suggest that either there is something wrong with the data or that each of the five toxic traits is so highly correlated with each other that no one trait has more significant influence over the others to find differences in influence on turnover intentions. Further investigation was undoubtedly required.

Table 7: Effects among Five Toxic Traits and Culture Typology

Dependent Variable: Turnover Intention

Source Type	df III Sum of Squares	Mean	Square	F	Sig.
Corrected Model	6487.767a	78	83.177	4.932	<.001
Intercept	74310.749	1	74310.749	4406.580	<.001
Self-Promotion	138.376	15	9.225	0.547	0.914
Abusive Supervision	155.010	15	10.334	0.613	0.866
Unpredictability	191.221	15	12.748	0.756	0.727
Narcissism	302.542	15	20.169	1.196	0.270
Authoritarian Leadership	312.031	15	20.802	1.234	0.242
Workplace Typology	337.327	3	112.442	6.668	<.001
Error	9005.156	534	16.864		
Total	201426.000	613			
Corrected Total	15492.923	612			

R Squared = .419 (Adjusted R Squared = .334)

Reviewing the Correlation between the Five Toxic Traits

Bivariate Correlations with All Five Toxic Traits. To test the correlation between the independent and dependent variables to verify the data, I completed a Bivariate Correlation to identify whether there was a significant correlation between each toxic leadership trait within the Toxic Leadership Scale (Schmidt, 2014) while including turnover intention. Using the Pearson 2- tailed correlation (p=<.001 showcases significance for a two-tailed test), I verified an extremely strong correlation between every toxic leadership trait and turnover intention.

When testing the self-promotion trait against the other variables, I found that the correlations were significant. For instance, self-promotion tested against abusive supervision had a correlation coefficient of .769 (p=<.001) based on n=613 observations, and self-promotion tested against unpredictability had a correlation coefficient of .771 (p=<.001) based on n=613 observations. Testing self-promotion against narcissism had a significance of .765 (r= .765, p=<.001), testing self-promotion against authoritarian leadership had a significance of .742 (r=.742, p=<.001), and self-promotion against turnover intention had a significance of .512 (r=.512, p=<.001); all based on n=613 observations. The results for every variable produced similar results, as shown in Table 8, showcasing a probable interdependent or a collinear relationship among the toxic leadership traits.

Table 8: Bivariate Correlations among Five Toxic Traits and Turnover Intention

		Self-Promotion.	Abusive Supervision	Unpredict-ability	Narcissism	Authoritarian Leadership	Turnover Intention
Self-Promotion	Pearson Correlation	1	.769**	.771**	.765**	.742**	.512**
	Sig. (2-tailed)		<.001	<.001	<.001	<.001	<.001
	N	613	613	613	613	613	613
Abusive Supervision.	Pearson Correlation	.769**	1	.835**	.803**	.799**	.491**
	Sig. (2-tailed)	<.001		<.001	<.001	<.001	<.001
	N	613	613	613	613	613	613
Unpredict-ability	Pearson Correlation	.771**	.835**	1	.832**	.815**	.530**
	Sig. (2-tailed)	<.001	<.001		<.001	<.001	<.001
	N	613	613	613	613	613	613
Narcissism	Pearson Correlation	.765**	.803**	.832**	1	.798**	.539**
	Sig. (2-tailed)	<.001	<.001	<.001		<.001	<.001
	N	613	613	613	613	613	613
Authoritarian Leadership	Pearson Correlation	.742**	.799**	.815**	.798**	1	.510**
	Sig. (2-tailed)	<.001	<.001	<.001	<.001		<.001
	N	613	613	613	613	613	613
Turnover Intention	Pearson Correlation	.512**	.491**	.530**	.539**	.510**	1
	Sig. (2-tailed)	<.001	<.001	<.001	<.001	<.001	
	N	613	613	613	613	613	613

**Correlation is significant at the p>.01 level (2-tailed).

Adding Culture Typology as a Moderating Variable

Univariate Model. Using a 2-way univariate general linear model, I wanted to analyze how the specific toxic leadership traits and their relationships with turnover intention would be affected by a moderating variable of culture typology. As shown in Table 9, there is a significant relationship between Self-Promotion (p=<.163) and turnover intention. The moderator had no effect. Table 10 verifies a significant correlation regarding the relationship between abusive supervision (p=<.474) and turnover intention when introducing culture typology as a moderating variable.

Table 9: Effects of Self-Promotion with Culture Typology as Moderating Variable

Dependent Variable: Turnover Intention

Source	Type III Sum of Squares	df	Mean Square	F	Sig.
Corrected Model	5564.420a	62	89.749	4.972	<.001
Intercept	82809.476	1	82809.476	4587.319	<.001
Workplace Typology	319.992	3	106.664	5.909	<.001
Self-Promotion	1389.950	15	92.663	5.133	<.001
Workplace* Self- Promotion	679.463	44	15.442	0.855	0.734
Error	9928.503	550	18.052		
Total	201426.000	613			
Corrected Total	15492.923	612			

R Squared = .359 (Adjusted R Squared = .287)

Table 10: Effects of Abusive Supervision with Culture Typology as Moderating Variable

Dependent Variable: Turnover Intention

Source	Type III Sum of Squares	df	Mean Square	F	Sig.
Corrected Model	5550.590a	61	90.993	5.043	<.001
Intercept	91834.803	1	91834.803	5089.447	<.001
Workplace Typology	361.847	3	120.616	6.684	<.001
Abusive Supervision	2067.531	15	137.835	7.639	<.001
Workplace Abusive Supervision	776.226	43	18.052	1.000	0.474
Error	9942.334	551	18.044		
Total	201426.000	613			
Corrected Total	15492.923	612			

R Squared = .358 (Adjusted R Squared = .287)

The trend continues, as shown in Table 11, with a significant correlation between the relationship of unpredictability (p=<.914) and turnover intention when introducing culture typology as a moderating variable. Table 12 verifies a significant correlation between the relationship of narcissism (p=<.991) and turnover intention when introducing culture typology as a moderating variable. Finally, Table 13 shows a significant correlation between authoritarian leadership (p<.405) and turnover intention, with culture typology as a moderating variable. The validity of the original toxic leadership scale may be unreliable when pulling apart individual traits to test against turnover intention with the moderating variable; however, it is worth it to verify the collinearity of the traits again.

Table 11: Effects of Unpredictability with Culture Typology as Moderating Variable

Dependent Variable: Turnover Intention

Source	Type III Sum of Squares	df	Mean Square	F	Sig.
Corrected Model	5737.639a	61	94.060	5.313	<.001
Intercept	99104.656	1	99104.656	5597.650	<.001
Workplace Typology	440.392	3	146.797	8.291	<.001
Unpredictability	2493.213	15	166.214	9.388	<.001
Workplace* Unpredictability	544.184	43	12.655	0.715	0.914
Error	9755.284	551	17.705		
Total	201426.000	613			
Corrected Total	15492.923	612			

R Squared = .370 (Adjusted R Squared = .301)

Table 12: Effects of Narcissism with Culture Typology as Moderating Variable

Dependent Variable: Turnover Intention

Source	Type III Sum of Squares	df	Mean Square	F	Sig.
Corrected Model	5754.831a	62	92.820	5.242	<.001
Intercept	81543.182	1	81543.182	4605.496	<.001
Workplace Typology	338.088	3	112.696	6.365	<.001
Narcissism	2433.844	15	162.256	9.164	<.001
Workplace* Narcissism	433.833	44	9.860	0.557	0.991
Error	9738.093	550	17.706		
Total	201426.000	613			
Corrected Total	15492.923	612			

R Squared = .371 (Adjusted R Squared = .301)

Table 13: Effects of Authoritarian Leadership with Culture Typology as Moderating Variable

Dependent Variable: Turnover Intention

Source	Type III Sum of Squares	df	Mean Square	F	Sig.
Corrected Model	5757.851a	61	94.391	5.342	<.001
Intercept	91737.986	1	91737.986	5192.322	<.001
Workplace Typology	453.009	3	151.003	8.547	<.001
Authoritarian Leadership	2630.564	15	175.371	9.926	<.001
Workplace* Authoritarian Leadership	790.099	43	18.374	1.040	0.405
Error	9735.073	551	17.668		
Total	201426.000	613			
Corrected Total	15492.923	612			

R Squared = .372 (Adjusted R Squared = .302)

Workplace Typology and Turnover Intention
Post Hoc Test of Workplace Typology. Workplace typology, as shown in Table 13, clearly affects Turnover Intention. In Table 14, I broke out the four workplace typologies to further analyze the relationships between each workplace and turnover intention. Again, Workplace 1 is identified as the Clan-culture typology; Workplace 2 is identified as the Hierarchical-culture typology; Workplace 3 is identified as the Market-culture typology; Workplace 4 is identified as the Adhocracy-culture typology (Cameron & Quinn, 1999).

Though leadership, and the toxic traits of those leaders, are more important than turnover intention, culture typology does have a role in whether an employee is more or less likely to want to leave their role. Taking out toxic leadership from the model, I found that specific workplaces are more likely to drive employee turnover intention than others. Employees working in Workplace 2 (Hierarchical-culture typology) and Workplace 3 (Market-culture typology), absent from a toxic leader, are more prone to leave their roles.

Table 14: Scheffe Post Hoc Test of Workplace Typology and Turnover Intention

Dependent Variable: Turnover Intention 95% Confidence Level

Which Workplace best fits your current organization?

Workplace	Mean Difference (i-j)	Std. Error	Sig.	Lower Bound	Upper Bound
Workplace (WP) 1 WP 2	-2.6596	0.37207	<.001	-3.7045	-1.6146
WP 3	-3.9543	0.51270	<.001	-5.3941	-2.5144
WP 4	-0.6110	0.58729	0.781	-2.2604	1.0383
Workplace (WP)2 WP 1	2.6596	0.37207	<.001	1.6146	3.7045
WP 3	-1.2947	0.51270	0.097	-2.7346	0.1452
WP 4	2.0485	0.58729	0.007	0.3992	3.6979
Workplace (WP)3 WP 1	3.9543	0.51270	<.001	2.5144	5.3941
WP 2	1.2947	0.51270	0.097	-0.1452	2.7346
WP 4	3.3432	0.68508	<.001	1.4192	5.2672
Workplace (WP)4 WP 1	0.6110	0.58729	0.781	-1.0383	2.2604
WP 2	-2.0485	0.58729	0.007	-3.6979	-0.3992
Wp 3	-3.3432	0.68508	,.001	-5.2672	-1.4192

Results

Revisiting the Research Questions

• Do each of the five toxic leadership traits significantly affect turnover intention?

• If so, are those effects modulated by cultural typologies?

Upon analysis completion, I was able to answer my two main research questions. Toxic leadership traits do have a significant effect on turnover intention. The data shows that each trait within the Toxic Leadership Scale (Schmidt, 2008) is highly correlated with turnover intention. That said, due to the extreme collinearity of the traits, it is impossible to analyze traits independently as each trait is overwhelmingly significant concerning the correlations with each other and their individual relationship with turnover intention.

When including the moderating variable of the four different culture typologies, according to Cameron and Quinn (1999), the strength of the toxic leadership traits is so great that it masks any culture typology modulating effects. However, if a toxic leader portraying the five toxic leadership traits (Schmidt, 2008) are taken out of the model, culture typology does affect turnover intention (i.e., dependent variable). There is a significant correlation between turnover intention and both Hierarchical-culture typologies and Market-based culture typologies.

Therefore, culture typology (i.e., moderating variable) does not have a moderating effect on turnover intention (i.e., dependent variable) when toxic leadership traits (i.e., independent variable) are involved due to the collinearity of the toxic leadership traits.

The testing results suggested clear answers to the null hypotheses as introduced in Chapter

1. Although it is challenging to provide which trait bears the most responsibility in leading to an employee's intent to turnover, each trait is undoubtedly responsible and affects such an intent. Therefore, I conclude that the analysis of this study rejects each of the null hypotheses that the toxic traits from Schmidt's (2008) study do not adversely affect the turnover intention of employees working in and of the four culture typologies.

Summary

In this chapter, I produced the analysis and the results from my study on the relationship between toxic leadership traits and employee turnover intention among the four cultural typologies. Using Momentive's survey platform and Momentive's Audience generator, I was able to collect research data from 613 participants. After completing the multiple regression analysis and multiple linear regression analysis, I have been able to answer my two research questions. Toxic leadership traits do have an extremely significant effect on turnover intention, and those effects are so strong that culture typology becomes irrelevant to an employee's intent to leave their role. The following, Chapter 5, discusses the impact of the current study's results, its application, and the way forward for future research.

Chapter 5: Discussion

The purpose of this quantitative cross-sectional non-experimental study was to determine if relationships exist between Schmidt's (2008) toxic leadership traits and Roodt's (2013) employee turnover intentions among participants working in one of four organizational culture typologies as identified by Cameron and Quinn (1999). There were two main questions regarding toxic leadership traits, the four cultural typologies, and employee turnover intentions I aimed to answer:

• Do each of the five toxic leadership traits significantly affect turnover intention?

• If so, are those effects moderated by cultural typologies?

The quantitative research method for this study was used to generalize the overall U.S. population (Albers, 2017). A total of 613 participants who were based in the United States, worked full-time in their current roles for at least one year, were subordinate to another individual (i.e., a leader), did not work at an executive level (i.e., C-suite) capacity, and who identified themselves as working within one of four cultural typologies defined by Cameron and Quinn (1999) were randomly chosen.

The survey was administered on the Momentive (formally SurveyMonkey) platform. The participants were recruited through Momentive's "Audience" feature, which provided access to the participant pool, and allowed for data collection, storage, and parsing. The results from this study suggested that toxic leadership traits have an extremely significant effect on turnover intention, and culture typologies have little to no overall effect on those relationships.

Interpretation of Findings

Correlation between the Five Toxic Traits Collectively

First, I intended to identify the strength between the toxic leadership traits as the independent variable identified in the Toxic Leadership Scale (Schmidt, 2014) and turnover intention as the dependent variable. A peculiar instance occurred in the initial test of the combined Toxic Leadership Scale of measurement against the turnover intention: None of the traits seemed to have a significant relationship to turnover intention. At first glance, the findings from this one test seemed to completely contradict Boddy's (2013) study on productivity and the wellbeing of an employee. Boddy found an employee working in a toxic environment resulting in disengagement and dissatisfaction would want to leave their role when it is most convenient. This initial test seemed to have contradicted the findings of Irvine and Evans' (1995) cross-section study on job satisfaction and turnover intention among nurses, where the nurses considered leaving their roles when the workplace became hostile and detrimental to their personal and professional wellbeing.

The initial test's outcome was unexpected, which pointed to either the data being flawed or the relationship between the traits and turnover intention being so strong that it overwhelmed the test itself. In the next few tests, the latter proved true. The traits were highly correlated and formulated a co-linear relationship proving both Boddy's (2013) study on productivity and wellbeing and Irvine and Evans' (1995) study on job satisfaction are in line with the findings of this study.

Correlation between the Five Toxic Traits Individually

The standard bivariate correlation was used to test the significance of each individual trait using the standard bivariate correlation against turnover intention as well as each other. Through this testing, the data proved accurate and without flaw, and each trait was highly correlated with other traits and the turnover intention. Essentially the results were so strong among the individual traits that the data provided a probable interdependent or a collinear relationship among the toxic leadership traits. Thus Schmidt's (2008) scale was once again validated, and each trait within the scale, such as (a) abusive supervision, (b) authoritarian leadership, (c) narcissism, (d) self- promotion, and (e) unpredictability, had a significant effect on turnover intention.

Narcissism, Self-Promotion, and Turnover Intention. The findings within the study allude to Simmons' (2020) work on the effect of narcissistic leaders on their subordinates, the self-promoting ideology of such leaders, and the resentment such leaders tend to exacerbate in followers through this trait. Chen et al. (2020) also concluded that a narcissistic leader would take credit when the outcome is positive but deflect criticism when the outcome is negative.

These actions, or lack thereof, tend to hinder an employee's confidence and self-esteem to the point of dulling an individual's go-getter attitude and zest for the work. Finally, Comey (2018) described a major downturn in employee morale when the two traits of such a leader were intermingled. The result was a hasty takeover of an entire culture leading to a slowdown in production and overall turnover. The findings provided evidence suggesting there was an extremely strong correlation between narcissism and the self-promoting of a leader, creating a hostile or toxic environment with turnover intention as aligned with the literature.

Abusive Supervision and Turnover Intention. Concerning abusive supervision, the findings of this study concluded that the strength of the significance of abusive behaviors and turnover intention is a reoccurring finding within the literature. These findings were in line with a study from Matos et al. (2018) regarding how cultures influenced by a leader's abusive behaviors may produce a greater outcome in the short term but tend to breed a culture based on fear inhibiting employees' production over time. A similar conclusion with a direct implication of an abusive leader found that fear, deceit, and anxiety demotivated employees and resulted in a near halt in productive behaviors (Seppalaa & Cameron, 2015). The hostility of such actions created an environment of obedience, exhausting subordinates and forcing either compliance or escape.

Authoritarian Leadership and Turnover Intention. The strength of an authoritarian leader and turnover intention found in this study is consistent with previous findings. Colquitt (2001), through their study on organizational justice, found that authoritarian leadership tends to rule consistently in the negative on those employees who do not succumb to the loyalty expectations of the leader and who often find themselves on the opposite side of their decisions. This lack of organizational justice, or equality in guidance, often dislodges trust within the culture and provides a backdrop of resentment and eventual turnover. Haslam et al. (2011), when reviewing the new psychology of leadership, also raised concerns the authoritarian leader-type with an un-wielding power could have on organizational culture and employee disengagement.

An authoritarian leader may have the ability to control an entire incentive and procedural process to ensure that those who show the highest loyalty receive the greatest gains (Rupp, 2011; Tepper, 2000).

Unpredictability and Turnover Intention. In this study, unpredictability was found to be strongly correlated with turnover intention. Among the literature, unpredictability is the common underlying theme in a dysfunctional organization. According to Johnson et al. (2016), unpredictability can help exacerbate an already stressed climate and create working conditions that lead to incivility that is parroted amongst coworkers. Concerning employee effectiveness, unpredictable leadership can cause a toxic environment that leaves employees emotionally exhausted, disengaged, and disenfranchised (Leet, 2011).

Toxic Traits, Turnover Intention, and Culture Typology

Finally, the data showed how the specific toxic leadership traits and their relationships with turnover intention were affected by a moderating variable of culture typology. In every instance, there was yet again a significant relationship between each toxic trait (Schmidt, 2008) and the intent of an employee to leave an organization (Roodt, 2013), even within the different culture typologies as portrayed in the Competing Values Framework (Cameron & Quinn, 1999). The analysis used the Toxic Leader Scale (Schmidt, 2014) as a full model and tested the individual traits separately.

The final findings concluded that there was no significant difference with or without the moderating variable and that the strength of the traits in relation to turnover intention was so strong that it essentially voided the various culture typologies altogether. Although none of the literature specifically stated this concept, some research has suggested that a toxic workplace culture may override any differences within the workplace itself. Bakkal et al. (2019) looked at the role of job satisfaction among toxic cultures and turnover intention and found that when toxicity persists, it usually voids the individual's satisfaction with the job itself. Within Governmental leadership, a similar sentiment with regard to toxic environments overrides the enjoyment of the position and can even affect those individuals outside of the organization if discussed in a wide-enough medium (Heppell, 2011). The evidence in this study along with the research suggests that toxic cultures may be so overwhelming that any type of variation in the workplace may have little to no effect on the overall outcome or betterment outside of direct intervention (Jahn, 2020; Leet, 2011).

Concluding the Data Analysis

During a study conducted in 2020, Chen et al. found that a narcissistic leader portraying varying forms of arrogance, self-promotion, and aggression towards employees severely impacted the employee culture, stirring fear, anxiety, and distrust (Chen et al., 2020). The results from Chen et al. were reflected in my study, suggesting that toxic workplace culture emphasizes an employee leaving the organization for a safer culture. To add, it is abundantly clear that the stress from such an environment does affect their work behavior, job satisfaction, morale and, ultimately, turnover, as suggested by Singh et al. (2018). My study further validated Schmidt's (2008) Toxic Leadership Scale. Finally, specific culture typologies based on Cameron and Quinn's (1999) work on workplace typologies may be relevant to external toxic leadership traits to turnover intention. However, when added as a moderating variable with the toxic leadership traits, the typologies are rendered irrelevant due to the overwhelming significance of the toxic traits.

Answering the Research Questions

There were two main questions I answered regarding toxic leadership traits, the four cultural typologies, and employee turnover intentions. These questions were mentioned throughout the research in various forms but were not specifically addressed or answered within the literature. Through the data collected, these questions have both been answered.

The first question: Do each of the five toxic leadership traits significantly affect turnover intention? The data emphatically suggests that the five toxic leadership traits (Schmidt, 2008) have a very strong influence on turnover intentions. The second question: If so, are those effects moderated by cultural typologies? The answer to this question is "no." As stated previously, the collinearity of the toxic leadership traits is so strong that those traits essentially void any modulating effect from any variations of Cameron and Quinn's (1999) four culture typologies.

As found in the literature review, there is little scientific analysis of understanding the phenomena of toxic leadership or toxic cultures with a moderating variable of specific culture typology. There are a few instances where toxic leadership overrides any mitigating or moderating factor. Bakkal et al. (2019) found that toxicity can void an individual's satisfaction with the job itself due to negative cultural sentiment. Heppell (2011) argued that a toxic leader could also negate an employee's love for the job, which can worsen the workplace culture. Flint and Webster (2011) attempted to curtail the effects of poor leadership on turnover intentions with an exit interview to pinpoint the problem, and the overwhelming majority pointed to a toxic culture driven by a toxic leader.

Even when creating the Turnover Intention Scale, Roodt (2013) recognized that a negative environment would certainly impact an employee's morale, and that impact would have an effect on whether or not the employee wishes to leave their role and the entity as a whole.

Roodt (2013) found that employees were so overwhelmed with the negativity and toxicity within the culture that the work was no longer the employees' function. Instead, the employee spent their time safeguarding themselves from possible inflicted harm, completely disengaging from the job.

Limitations

The study was not all-encompassing and had some gaps that were not explored due to various constraints such as time, scale, and compartmentalization (i.e., the focus of the topic). I wanted to verify the strength of the toxic leadership traits on turnover intentions while also learning which traits of the toxic leadership scale (Schmidt, 2014) are perceived the most detrimental and whether there are other possible moderating effects of a toxic culture, such as demographics or type of work. These limitations within this study are further discussed in this section.

Original Intent

Initially, I set out to explore whether I could quantify which toxic leadership traits, if any, were more detrimental to employees' job satisfaction compared to other traits using Roodt's (2013) Turnover Intention Scale (TIS-6) to determine the effects on the dependent variable of turnover intentions. Once again, the correlation among the traits is simply too strong on their own and as a collective within the entirety of Schmidt's (2014) Toxic Leadership Scale. Testing those relationships with a moderating variable of Cameron's and Quinn's (1999) culture typology did not change the overall outcome. The toxic traits provided overwhelming evidence for the validity of Schmidt's Toxic Leadership Scale, the significance of the traits concerning turnover intention, and the irrelevance of typology as a moderating factor or variable.

Demographics as a Factor

Although demographics were collected from the participants, the data was not used within the analysis. Responses to demographic questions identified age, gender, level of education, time in the current role, and ethnicity. The decision not to differentiate between or analyze specific characteristics prevented me from distinguishing the differences and nuances between these factors.

The study also collected minimal data on the various workplaces, such as a corporate or private sector, government or public sector, or within a military environment, but did not differentiate toxic leadership types within those workplaces. The information collected was briefly viewed but discarded for inconsistent participant answers and skewed data. Multiple past studies viewed toxicity through these specific lenses, such as Boddy's (2013) work on corporate psychopaths reviewing the phenomena that created counterproductive work behavior, Reed's (2004, 2015) view on toxicity in military cultures, and the various work on toxic cultures within the public sector (Comey, 2018; Heppell, 2011). Given the overwhelming correlation among the traits, it is possible that demographics would play a major role in the overall outcome.

Implications

Dark or toxic leadership is an astounding array of hostility that stems from a minority and greatly affects the majority. In this researcher's opinion, and as stated in previous chapters, the study of such leadership and its effect on a culture is still lacking in both depth and context. I believe the scientific community studying human behavior in organizational settings has much more work to do studying this phenomenon. The community owes not only organizations and human resources adequate scientific data but our society the tools it needs to hold toxic leaders accountable and help mend these broken cultures.

One of the goals for the organizations may be to help alleviate the extreme monetary implications of toxic leadership that cost the overall economy billions annually (Bouchey & Glynn, 2012; Jahn, 2020; McClear, 2019). Perhaps these entities mean to improve morale through the various implications of positive leadership (Arthur & Hardy, 2014; Audi & Murphy, 2006; Haslam et al., 2011). Or maybe these entities simply want to increase fairness in an already lopsided economic arrangement about organizational justice (Colquitt, 2001; Hoppe, 2007; Northouse, 2013; Rupp, 2011). No matter the reasoning for organizations to change their practices, those studying behavior organizations can assist them.

Theoretical Implications

This study's theoretical findings are consistent with the overall theme provided by Schmidt's Toxic Leadership Scale (2008) and Schmidt's (2014) subsequent work on toxic leadership and the resulting effects beyond the victims and the toll each trait exults on the culture. Researchers have studied the effects of such leadership on job satisfaction and have provided several key findings from studies on the overall outcome of job dissatisfaction linking the phenomena to both toxic leadership and turnover intention (Bakkal et al., 2019; Irvine & Evans, 1995; Roodt, 2013). A resounding effect can plague an entire entity and cause irreparable harm to the organization, its customers, and its people. This study offers some clarity to the current science and modest gains in the knowledge gaps found in the current body of literature.

Practical Implications

This study also has practical implications. Understanding the cost of such leadership provided by the previous case studies on the monetary business impact of poor workplace culture (Sorenson & Garman, 2013; Stiroh, 2018) is a start. Using that knowledge and expanding on the impact of a toxicity-laden environment via the relationship between employee engagement and job satisfaction towards productivity (Tampubolon, 2016) allows Human Resource Management and senior leaders to realize tangible losses of such cultures. Using past research and this study's findings, the new data and the revalidation of past data can help codify current workplaces or organizational cultures by providing a scientific backdrop to help mitigate the promotion or hiring of a toxic leader. This study can also help HRM and other professionals identify a poor, dark, or toxic environment.

Future Research

This study has implications that affect workplaces from both a theoretical and practical standpoint. However, there is still more work to be done to understand these implications. In this researcher's purview, several study expansions should occur to help further fill gaps in knowledge. Industrial-organizational scientists need to continue to keep striving for more data and more knowledge. The findings of this study can help identify a toxic leader and/or toxic environment. That said, I think it is prevalent that future researchers try to identify ways to remediate the adverse effects of these leaders and cultures. Finally, an unintended outcome provided an interesting data point that suggested that the workplace typology may be a catalyst for turnover. This interesting yet small piece of information was not fully analyzed nor dissected but could lead to further knowledge on preferred cultures or types of individuals that prefer specific typologies and may tend to depart their roles early.

Remedial Action for Toxic Leaders

While creating this study proposal, I also wanted to know if remedial actions existed and, if so, what they look like. There are implications to toxic leadership and how those implications affect the overall picture of an entity. However, perhaps that could have been a way to save Merril Lynch from its leader's ego and unpredictability (Farrell, 2011). Perhaps a method could have alleviated the workers of Wells Fargo from its leader's sales aggression and abusive supervision (Ferrel & Ferrel, 2017). Or maybe remedial strategies would have saved Enron from its leaders' greed and narcissism (McLean & Elkind, 2013).

Such actions could help stymy or even defeat toxic leadership, thus saving employees from becoming subject to an extreme environment they seemingly cannot escape (Ferrel & Ferrel, 2017; Singh et al., 2018). Or, as past research had suggested, they are forced to escape while putting their financial stability on the line just to feel personal safety or security (Lipman- Blumen, 2005). I do not doubt that future studies will provide data on how to thwart such leaders and their impulses and maybe even repair caused damages. Finally, future studies will be able to answer whether a curriculum can be developed and applied in a corporate, government, or even military setting.

Culture Typology May Lead to Turnover Intention by Itself

Culture typology was initially meant to be tested as the moderating variable within the study. The intent was to see if a different workplace typology would affect the relationship between toxic leadership and turnover intention. However, while verifying the strength of the relationship by testing narcissism and authoritarian leadership (Schmidt, 2008), with turnover intention (Roodt, 2013) as the dependent variable, I curiously added culture typology as another independent variable (Cameron & Quinn, 1999).

Through this test, I found that culture typology itself can be a catalyst for turnover intention. Although the literature does not provide scientific insight into this phenomenon, it is clear there is a significant relationship, and the relationship seems to vary amongst the four different typologies of Cameron and Quinn (1999). The outcome was unexpected and should lead to future studies by testing each typology individually with turnover intention as the dependent variable to provide further data.

Conclusion

The purpose of this quantitative cross-sectional non-experimental study was to determine if relationships exist between Schmidt's (2008) toxic leadership traits and Roodt's (2013) employee turnover intentions among participants working in one of four organizational culture typologies as defined by Cameron and Quinn (1999). Through this study, I was able to answer in the affirmative that toxic leaderships traits do have a significant effect on turnover intentions yet to the negative, that culture typologies do not seem to moderate those relationships due to the nature of the strength of the latter's relationship with turnover intention and the correlation between the individual traits themselves.

In this chapter, I discussed the study's limitations, the implications of the findings, and how those implications affect the theory of organizational science. I discussed the implications and applications of the findings for practical use. I also discussed what steps should be taken to help cover continued knowledge gaps in the science and potential future research.

Toxic leaders cripple economies, dismantle corporate giants, and drive narratives that decimate the reputations of entire countries. That said, progress does not stop for anyone, and as we move along in the evolution of thought on psychological sciences in a collective sense, we must also move along in an organizational sense. Identifying what toxic leadership is and how it affects a culture (whether corporate or Government) through data is how we begin to correct a global problem and work towards a better and brighter future where everyone can participate freely and without fear.

References

Albers, M. J. (2017). *Introduction to quantitative data analysis in the behavioral and social sciences.* John Wiley & Sons.

American Psychological Association. (2017). *Ethical principles of psychologists and code of conduct.* https://www.apa.org. https://www.apa.org/ethics/code.

Arthur, C., & Hardy, L. (2014). Transformational leadership: A quasi-experimental study. *Leadership & Organization Development Journal, 35*(1), 38-53.

Audi, R., & Murphy, P. E. (2006). The many faces of integrity. *Business Ethics Quarterly, 16*(1), 3-21. https://www.cambridge.org/core/journals/business-ethics-quarterly/article/abs/many-faces-of-integrity/B4C19715364A91769ED9A59655A04AAB.

Bakkal, E., Serener, B., & Myrvang, N. A. (2019). Toxic leadership and turnover intention: Mediating role of job satisfaction. *Revista de Cercetare si Interventie Sociala, 66*, 88-102.https://www.researchgate.net/publication/335850849_Toxic_Leadership_and_Turno ver_Intention_Mediating_Role_of_Job_Satisfaction.

Boddy, C. R. (2013). Corporate psychopaths, conflict, employee affective wellbeing and counterproductive work behaviour. *Journal of Business Ethics, 121*(1), 107-121. https://www.researchgate.net/publication/257542238_Corporate_Psychopaths_Conflict_ Employee_Affective_Well-Being_and_Counterproductive_Work_Behaviour.

Boogaard, K. (2022). The 4 Types of Company Culture, Explained. https://www.atlassian.com/blog/teamwork/types-of-corporate-culture.

Borgatta, E., Bales, R., & Couc, A. O. (1954). Some findings relevant to the great man theory of leadership. *American Sociological Review.*

Bouchey, H., & Glynn, S. (2012, November 16). There are significant business costs to replacing employees. *Center for American Progress.* https://www.americanprogress.org/issues/economy/reports/2012/11/16/44464/there-are- significant-business-costs-to-replacing-employees/.

Burchett, D., & Ben-Porath, Y. S. (2019). Methodological considerations for developing and evaluating response bias indicators. *Psychological Assessment, 31*(12), 1497-1511. https://pubmed.ncbi.nlm.nih.gov/31763874/.

Cameron, K. (2017, October 31). Managing competing values. *BYU Wheatley Institution.*https://wheatley.byu.edu/managing-competing-values/.

Cameron, K. S., & Quinn, R. E. (1999). Diagnosing and changing organizational culture: Based on the Competing Values Framework. Addison-Wesley.

Celebi, N., Guner, H., & Yıldız, V. (2015). *Development of a Leadership Scale.* Barton University, (4)2, 249-268. Bartın, Turkey.

Chen, J., Cheng, Z., Wang, H., & Li, D. (2020). Does leader narcissism hinder employees taking charge? An affective events theory perspective. *Social Behavior and Personality: An International Journal, 48*(10), 1-13. https://www.sbp-journal.com/index.php/sbp/article/view/9377.

Colquitt, J. A. (2001). On the dimensionality of organizational justice: A construct validation of a measure. *Journal of Applied Psychology, 86*(3), 386-400. https://psycnet.apa.org/record/2001-06715-002.

Comey, J. (2018). *A higher loyalty: Truth, lies, and leadership.* Flatiron Books.

Denison, D. (2019). Introduction to the Denison model. *Denison Consulting.* https://www.denisonconsulting.com/wp-content/uploads/2019/08/introduction-to-the- denison-model.pdf.

Down, R. (2019, March 12). Adhocracy culture: Pros and cons. https://www.breathehr.com/en- gb/blog/topic/company-culture/adhocracy-culture-pros-and-cons.

Farrell, G. (2011). *Crash of the titans: Greed, hubris, the fall of Merrill Lynch, and the near- collapse of Bank of America.* Crown Publication.

Faul, F., Erdfelder, E., Lang, A., & Buchner, A. (2007). G*Power 3: A flexible statistical power analysis program for the social, behavior, and biomedical sciences. *Behavior Research Methods, 39*(1), 175-191.

Ferrel, O., & Ferrel, L. (2017, August 31). Wells Fargo's organizational culture: Can you bank on it? https://harbert.auburn.edu/research-faculty/centers/center-for-ethical- organizational-cultures/wellsfargo.html.

Flint, A., & Webster, J. (2011). The use of the exit interview to reduce turnover amongst healthcare professionals. *Cochrane Database of Systematic Reviews.* https://www.ncbi.nlm.nih.gov/pmc/articles/PMC7390136/#:~:text=In%2

0theory%2C%2

0the%20exit%20interview,amenable%20to%20quality%20improve-
ment%20activities.

Gligor, D. M., Holcomb, M. C., & Stank, T. P. (2013). A multidisciplinary approach to supply chain agility: Conceptualization and scale development. *Journal of Business Logistics, 34*(2), 94-108. https://onlinelibrary.wiley.com/doi/abs/10.1111/jbl.12012.

Haslam, S. A., Reicher, S. D., & Platow, M. J. (2011). *The new psychology of leadership: Identity, influence and power.* Psychology Press.

Heppell, T. (2011). Toxic leadership: Applying the Lipman-Blumen model to political leadership. *Representation, 47*(3), 241-249. https://www.tandfonline.com/doi/abs/10.1080/00344893.2011.596422.

Hoe, J., & Hoare, Z. (2013). Understanding quantitative research: Part 1. *Nursing Standard, 27*(15-17), 52-57. http://rcnpublishing.com/journal/ns.

Hoppe, M. (2007). Culture and leader effectiveness: The GLOBE study. http://www.inspireimagineinnovate.com/pdf/globesummary-by-michael-h-hoppe.pdf.

IBM. (2022). SPSS software. IBM - United States. https://www.ibm.com/analytics/spss- statistics-software.

Irvine, D. M., & Evans, M. G. (1995). Job satisfaction and turnover among nurses: Integrating research findings across studies. *Nursing Research, 44*(4), 246-253. https://psycnet.apa.org/record/1996-09787-001.

Isaacson, W. (2015). *Steve Jobs.* Simon & Schuster.

Jahn, E. (2020, December 3). The cost of employee disengagement. *Xactly.* https://www.xactlycorp.com/blog/cost-disengagement-turnover.

Johnson, R., Rosen, C., Gabriel, A., & Koopman, J. (2016). How incivility spreads in the workplace. *Journal of Applied Psychology.* https://www.sciencedaily.com/releases/2016/08/160810104409.htm.

Koocher, G. P. (2013). Ethical considerations in clinical psychology research. *Oxford Handbooks Online.* https://academic.oup.com/edited-volume/34403/chapter- abstract/296623919?redirectedFrom=fulltext.

Lazarczyk, L. (2017, June 14). Life meets work survey finds 56% of employees have a toxic leader. markets.businessinsider.com. https://markets.businessinsider.com/news/stocks/life-meets-work-survey-finds-56-of- employees-have-a-toxic-leader-1001767434.

Leet, E. (2011). *The impact toxic or severe dysfunctional leadership has on the effectiveness of an organization.* Murdoch University.

Lindebaum, D., & Cartwright, S. (2010). A critical examination of the relationship between emotional intelligence and transformational leadership. *Journal of Management Studies.* https://onlinelibrary.wiley.com/doi/full/10.1111/j.1467-6486.2010.00933.x.

Lipman-Blumen, J. (2005). The allure of toxic leaders: Why followers rarely escape their clutches or the paradox of toxic leadership. *Ivey Business Journal.* https://assess.connectiveleadership.com/documents/why_followers_rarely_escape_their_ clutches.pdf.

Marshall, A., & Batten, S. (2004). Researching across cultures: Issues of ethics and Power. *Qualitative Sozialforschung.* https://www.qualitative-research.net/index.php/fqs/article/view/572/1241.

Matos, K., O'Neill, O. M., & Lei, X. (2018). Toxic leadership and the masculinity contest culture: How "win or die" cultures breed abusive leadership. *Journal of Social Issues, 74*(3), 500-528. https://spssi.onlinelibrary.wiley.com/doi/abs/10.1111/josi.12284.

Mawritz, M. B., Mayer, D. M., Hoobler, J. M., Wayne, S. J., & Marinova, S. V. (2012). A trickle-down model of abusive supervision. *Personnel Psychology, 65*(2), 325-357.

McClear, S. (2019, October 8). Toxic workplaces have costs businesses $223 billion over the last 5 years. *Ladders.* https://www.theladders.com/career-advice/toxic-workplaces-have- costs-businesses-223-billion-in-turnover-over-the-last-five-years.

McLean, B., & Elkind, P. (2013). *The smartest guys in the room: The amazing rise and scandalous fall of Enron.* Penguin.

McLeod, S. (2019). Qualitative vs. Quantitative Research. [online] Simplypsychology.org. https://www.simplypsychology.org/qualitative-quantitative.html.

Momentive. (2021). Why use Momentive. https://www.momentive.com Northouse, P. G. (2013). Trait approach. http://www.sagepub.com/upm-data/30933_Northouse_Chapter_2.pdf.

Reed, G. (2004). Toxic leadership. *Military Review,* 67-71. http://www.george-reed.com/uploads/3/4/4/5/34450740/toxic_leadership.pdf.

Reed, G. (2015). *Tarnished: Toxic leadership in the U.S. military*. University of Nebraska Press.

Resick, C. J., Hargis, M. B., Shao, P., & Dust, S. B. (2013). Ethical leadership, moral equity judgments, and discretionary workplace behavior. *Human Relations, 66*(7), 951-972. doi:10.1177/0018726713481633.

Roodt, G. (2004). Turnover intentions. Unpublished document. Johannesburg: University of Johannesburg.

Roodt, G. (2013). The validation of the turnover intention scale. *Journal of Human Resource Management, 11*(1), 12.
https://journals.co.za/doi/abs/10.4102/sajhrm.v11i1.507.

Rosen, C. C., Koopman, J., Gabriel, A. S., & Johnson, R. E. (2016). Who strikes back? A daily investigation of when and why incivility begets incivility. *Journal of Applied Psychology, 101*(11), 1620-1634.

RunMeetly. (2021, January 28). The four types of organizational cultures.
https://www.runmeetly.com/four-types-organizational-culture.

Rupp, D. (2011). An employee-centered model of organizational justice and social responsibility. *Organizational Psychology Review, 1*(1), 72-94. https://journals.sagepub.com/doi/abs/10.1177/2041386610376255.

Sahlqvist, S., Song, Y., Bull, F., Adams, E., Preston, J., & Ogilvie, D. (2011). Effect of questionnaire length, personalisation and reminder type on response rate to a complex postal survey: Randomised controlled trial. *BMC Medical Research Methodology, 11*(1).
https://link.springer.com/article/10.1186/1471-2288-11-62.

Savage-Austin, A. R., & Honeycutt, A. (2011). Servant leadership: A phenomenological study of practices, experiences, organizational effectiveness, and barriers. *Journal of Business & Economics Research (JBER), 9*(1). https://www.clute-journals.com/index.php/JBER/article/view/939.

Schlaegel, C., Engle, R. L., & Lang, G. (2020). The unique and common effects of emotional intelligence dimensions on job satisfaction and facets of job performance: An exploratory study in three countries. *The International Journal of Human Resource Management*, 1-44.
https://www.tandfonline.com/doi/full/10.1080/09585192.2020.1811368

Schmidt, A. (2008). Development and validation of the toxic leadership scale.
http://hdl.handle.net/1903/8176

Schmidt, A. (2014). An examination of toxic leadership, job outcomes, and the impact of military deployment. http://hdl.handle.net/1903/15250.

Selya, A. S., Rose, J. S., Dierker, L. C., Hedeker, D., & Mermelstein, R. J. (2012). A practical guide to calculating Cohen's f2, a measure of local effect size, from PROC MIXED. *Frontiers in Psychology.* https://doi.org/10.3389/fpsyg.2012.00111.

Seppalaa, E., & Cameron, K. (2015, December 1). Proof that positive work cultures are more productive. *Harvard Business Review.* https://hbr.org/2015/12/proof-that-positive-work- cultures-are-more-productive.

SHRM. (2021, February 24). Organizational culture. https://www.shrm.org/ResourcesAndTools/Pages/Organizational-Culture.aspx.

Simmons, L. (2020, April 30). How narcissistic leaders destroy from within. https://www.gsb.stanford.edu/insights/how-narcissistic-leaders-destroy-within.

Singh, N., Sengupta, S., & Dev, S. (2018). Toxic leadership: The most menacing form of leadership. Dark sides of organizational behavior and leadership.

Sorenson, S., & Garman, K. (2013). How to tackle U.S. employees' stagnating engagement. *Business Journal.* https://news.gallup.com/businessjournal/162953/tackle- employees-stagnating-engagement.aspx.

Stiroh, K. (2018, March 22). The economics of why companies don't fix their toxic cultures. *Harvard Business Review.* https://hbr.org/2018/03/the-economics-of-why-companies- dont-fix-their-toxic-cultures.

Sudjiwanati, N., & Pinastikasari, N. (2020). Employee performance and employee engagement towards job satisfaction. *Proceedings of the International Conference on Community Development* (ICCD 2020). https://www.atlantis-press.com/proceedings/iccd- 20/125945168.

Tampubolon, H. (2016). The relationship between employee engagement, job motivation, and job satisfaction towards the employee performance. *Corporate Ownership and Control, 13*(2), 473-477. http://repository.uki.ac.id/624/.

Tavakol, M., & Dennick, R. (2021). Making sense of Cronbach's Alpha. *PubMed Central (PMC).* https://www.ncbi.nlm.nih.gov/pmc/articles/PMC4205511/.

Tepper, B. J. (2000). Consequences of abusive supervision. *Academy of Management Journal, 43*(2), 178-190. doi:10.5465/1556375.

Tepper, B. J., Duffy, M. K., Hoobler, J., & Ensley, M. D. (2004). Moderators of the relationships between coworkers' organizational citizenship behavior and fellow employees' attitudes. *Journal of Applied Psychology, 89(3)*, 455-465

www.ingramcontent.com/pod-product-compliance
Lightning Source LLC
Chambersburg PA
CBHW071341130726
47996CB00002B/805